Leveraging Your
HIGH STAKES PRESENTATION
in the Age of Speed

Persuasive Presentation Techniques
including a Laser Blueprint Methodology

Kendall Hunt
publishing company

Robert Petrausch
Iona College

Cover images © Shutterstock.com

www.kendallhunt.com
Send all inquiries to:
4050 Westmark Drive
Dubuque, IA 52004-1840

Copyright © 2020 by Kendall Hunt Publishing Company

Printed text and KHQ ISBN 978-1-7924-3283-5
eBook and KHQ ISBN 978-1-7924-0534-1

Published in the United States of America

CONTENTS

Overview: Leveraging High-Stakes Presentations in the Age of Speed

This book provides a **LASER** proprietary blueprint for professionals to prepare, deliver, and win high-stakes presentations in the age of speed. It offers advice and tools on how to **leverage** your talk, **adapt** to your audiences needs and analytics, **share** your ideas with key stakeholders, **educate** stakeholders with powerful stories, and **reveal** novel solutions. This book focuses on the demands that the age of speed exerts on professionals and has the tools, brainstorming strategies, and methods to wow and win audiences with new ideas, powerful stories, checklists, and innovative approaches to fast-track a presentation. It also provides new approaches to advance the careers of high-stakes presenters and make influential decision makers want to advance your crucial agendas, whether in sales, public relations, advertising, policy advocacy, fundraising, marketing, branding, science/technology, or other professional areas of interest.

Most books on presentations give one the fundamentals to prepare and deliver general presentations, but lack an analytical blueprint to help fast-track the high-stakes presentation. While the book is essential for professionals in business, communications, nonprofit organizations, the arts, and the military, it also addresses the presentation needs of scientists and technologists who must share their ideas with high-level decision makers. Students who are preparing for careers in a professional field will find the book a useful resource to fast-track their careers.

Professionals will want to embrace this book because it provides a smooth and seamless process for crafting and delivering high-stakes presentations and advancing their careers.

Book Specs and Features

The Laser Code: Leveraging, +Adapting+ Sharing +Educating+ Revealing= High-Stakes Presentation Blueprint. It includes samples of high-stakes presentations, checklists, and chapter summaries that are easy to remember and follow.

Benefits for the Reader

1. Provides a Laser blueprint to fast-track presentations
2. Includes tools and methods to make a memorable presentation
3. Explains how TED Talks and Shark Tank presentations can help improve your high-stakes presentations
4. Provides advice to advance and jump-start your career
5. Describes how to work on and succeed with a team presentation
6. Suggests new ways to use new presentation tech tools to deliver your presentation in the age of speed.
7. Enables readers to learn and practice the latest persuasion tools for audience buy-in.
8. Provides useful exercises to improve their communications and public speaking skills.

About the Author

Dr. Robert J. Petrausch, an expert in communications, is head of the Public Relations concentration and former chair of the Department of Mass Communication at Iona College in New Rochelle, NY. He started his career in public relations and organizational communication following a period of service as a captain in the United States Air Force. He has held key positions in public relations and organizational communication with Shell Oil, General Electric, Sperry Corporation, and GTE and served as top communications executive for Uniroyal Chemical in Middlebury, CT. He has a master's degree in public relations from Boston University, a Master of Arts degree in political science from Fordham University, a master's degree in liberal studies from the New School for Social Research, and a doctoral degree in education from Columbia University with a focus on organization and leadership.

Dr. Petrausch has a broad background in speech writing, public relations, internal communications, media relations, program planning, organizational communication and learning, public relations, and management/training. He provides consulting advice to executives from Fortune 1000 companies and nonprofit organizations. He is a past president and board member of the Westchester-Fairfield Chapter of the Public Relations Society of America. He holds membership in the Association for Education in Journalism and Mass Communication and the Public Relations Society of America and serves on the board of the CT Chapter of the United Nations Association. He has also served on the National Board of the United Nations Association-USA. Dr. Petrausch is a member of the Princeton Club in New York.

High-Stakes Presentations in the Age of Speed

If everything seems under control, you are not going fast enough.

—Mario Andretti

L earning to harness speed is the one accomplishment that can catapult you and your organization to new heights in the digital age. The electronic speed of all our devices has made it easier to capture information, post it, and spread it virally. A smart professional must learn new tools to advance ideas that will help sway influential decision makers, the subject of this book.

New ideas are often thwarted because the noise of communication in society clamors for our attention, and the flood of new information hampers the creative professional from sorting out the best ideas and approaches from any given presentation, especially the high-stakes presentation, a presentation whose primary aim is to persuade influential decision makers to adopt your program, cause, or proposal.

So why do we worship speed and velocity? The answer is simple: We want to run, ride, and think faster. Each new generation seems to want to go faster than the previous one. In the United States, we have speed dating, speed checkouts, and even speed bosses. Europe and Asia have fast bullet trains, fast biking (Tour de France), and even fast speed skating. If you watch movies and TV shows from a decade ago, you will notice that the dialogue and action scenes moved much more slowly than they do now.

Studies from around the world have shown that the pace of physical movement increases with the size of the city. Walk in New York City, Paris, or Berlin, and then visit their suburbs or rural areas, and the great difference in speed will become immediately noticeable.

The media sound bite has dropped from about forty seconds in 1968 to about seven seconds in 2017. Political sound bites are also much shorter, as witnessed in recent US and European elections. Even commercial slogans are following the NIKE model of "Just Do It." What is more, our sentences are shorter today than in previous generations.

Speeding images and messages in movies and TV flash before our eyes, trying to capture our attention and make us take notice. Persuasive messages have grown exponentially and are changing constantly on social media platforms, as exhibited by the now famous emoticons.

With all this speed engulfing us incessantly, we still seem to prepare our high-stakes presentations with antiquated tools and written materials, forgetting that the blend of information, entertainment, and persuasive influence needs to be part of a twenty-first century high-stakes presentation.

Why I Wrote This Book

As a former air force officer and chief communications officer for a Fortune 500 company, I had the responsibility to prepare high-level presentations that would influence important decision makers and key stakeholders in the military and commercials sectors of society. No matter where I searched, however, I rarely found presentation books for the high-stakes presenter; it seemed that most authors were aiming at the general presenters and ignoring those who had to make serious or competitive presentations. Some books with topics such as talking to the top people or winning presentation styles surfaced and were pretty good, but most missed the mark, and I was essentially on my own. Analog-age tools and commentary still ruled the presentation book genre. So now with more time for research as an academic, I had a chance to recall and put into practice what I learned at Boston University's School of Communication and Columbia University's Department of Organization and Leadership and from my helpful colleagues in academia. My air force and corporate experience added an important perspective to this book. With all this insight, I decided to develop a proprietary blueprint methodology that the high-stakes presenter could use to create a presentation alone or with a team.

The Laser Code methodology provides the framework for the high-stakes presentation, and its five-step process will help fast-track the presentation with new tools and approaches that make sense for the age of speed. This new book is created to help you capture and brainstorm ideas for your high-stakes presentation and to work successfully with new presentation technology as well as traditional and social media.

As we move more quickly into the age of speed, the ubiquitous nature of digital communications and its click society are changing the way we communicate from the big screen to the small screens of our digital devices, making it necessary to make messages resonate at a faster pace than in the past. The digital format is making us work more with video, audio, and symbolic images just as a producer might do with a movie. In short, we are now a part of the hyperconnected world. The learning takeaway from the new digital communications paradigm is that your message will not make any headway unless you get it into a format that your audience has a comfortable connection with.[1]

Some companies such as Amazon are now insisting that their employees write narratives instead of PowerPoint presentations. PowerPoint, however, for all its benefits and limitations, is still the presentation tool of choice for many organizations. Whether or not you use PowerPoint, the packaging of your presentation is very important for getting noticed in a hyperconnected, noisy communications environment. Your content now needs to be packaged with video, audio, and data so that it is easy to remember and retain.

The visual image along with strong supporting information and data will most likely be the dominant way to make the case with influential decision makers associated with high-stakes presentations. An added proviso: To keep your ideas salient in the high-stakes presentation, the visuals and content must be connected to a strong emotional component. The famous adage still holds: "People buy with emotion and justify with facts."[2]

In most presentations, and in particular the high-stakes presentation, leaders are often the driving force because they typically steer the presentation with the force of their personality, their credibility within the organization, and their genuine empathy for the people who work for them. Take a look at how Lou Gerstner of IBM fame helped change the culture of his organization through his leadership approach of teaching the elephant to dance, the namesake of his business book that went on to become a best seller. Gerstner had to deliver a number of high-stakes presentations to the IBM leaders and employees to help them change direction and stay alive as a company. He moved the company from manufacturing to service and infused an entrepreneurial mindset into an IBM culture that had failed to adapt to the technological changes in

© Billion Photos/Shutterstock.com

© Adier Romero/Shutterstock.com

the computer industry. According to many analysts, he performed a business miracle by making sure everybody—employees, customers, and stakeholders—got his message without dismantling the company's spirit and drive.

In Chapter 4, we will examine in more detail how leaders share ideas and achieve buy-in, moving the organization ahead with important high-stakes presentations. Selling ideas to an internal audience can be exceedingly challenging for the following reasons:

1. Competing camps in the organization can change your ideas.
2. Other projects may compete for the scarce resources and funding in organizations.
3. The needs of key stakeholders and managers are more important than the leaders' own personal needs and goals.

Once the leader moves in the direction to address the real, instead of peripheral, needs of management, the chances for success are dramatically improved. This piece of advice is particularly important in the high-stakes presentation where connecting with influential decision makers is critical. Although the leader drives the message, the formal high-stakes presentation itself is the moment of truth when you need to close the multimillion-dollar sale or make a case to a congressional committee, professional group, or board of directors.

The ancients, particularly Aristotle, had some important things to say about persuasion in a presentation. For one thing, Aristotle was convinced that no matter how compelling your case, facts alone would not get your audience to pay attention. Yet many presenters insist on overloading their presentations, including PowerPoints, with facts and not much else. This tactic is a disaster for most presenters, particularly the high-stakes presenter.

For Aristotle ethos, logos, and pathos are the three elements of argument. Ethos is about your credibility

© Svetlana Mahovskaya./Shutterstock.com

as a speaker and the credibility of the organization that you represent. Low credibility translates into a failure to communicate. Logos is the logic and organizing principle of your message. You must be able to take your audience on a journey from point A to B to C and keep them interested. Pathos is the emotional component of the message. The audience must feel that you care about them and that you are passionate about the topic of your talk.[3] As noted, effective communications must be anchored in the emotions of the audience and must be tailored to their terms and not yours.

The basic rules of Aristotle hold true today in the age of speed. High-stakes influencers and decision makers may want instant information, but they care more about the credibility of the speaker, whether he or she has presented a compelling logical case, and, of course, his or her passion for the topic.

The true test of an effective high-stakes presentation is how well the presenter "front loads" the talk with the most important information, a finding borne out in rhetorical and psychological research. This approach puts the critical takeaways from the presentation at the forefront of the listener's mind. He or she can see right away the direction the speaker is going and the importance of the key messages. A talk with the most important information first also prevents the audience from waiting a long time to get to the heart of the presentation and from getting bored before the speech is over. Finally, this approach keeps up the momentum started by the presenter and provides a reason for the audience to keep listening, a vital necessity in the age of speed.

A tool for front-loading the talk is delivering a powerful headline that grabs the attention of the audience. Simply asking yourself or your team what matters the most to this audience will give the speaker the clues he or she needs to find the right headline for the audience. Often what matters most is the elephant-in-the-room topic that most are refusing to address. Many professionals make the mistake of trying to smooth over the difficult topic or save it for another time. If you nail the big idea early in the presentation, your listeners will reward you for not wasting their time.[4]

Besides nailing the big idea upfront in your presentation, you need to create a communication experience that is important to your listeners. This experience will help create the audience connection that is critical to your success, a connection that shows that you care about, respect, and understand what the audience really needs. You should be prepared to use stories, analogies, and, in some cases, humor to make your point.

Let's be realistic and understand that your big ideas must be sold, and the audience must willingly accept your proposals in order for them to move forward. Selling to the top people is even more important in the age of speed.

The saying that "nothing happens until someone sells something" is absolutely true. It makes sense to recognize that some ideas are more likely to advance than others; therefore, the presenter must choose carefully the ideas to include up front and move forward in the high-stakes presentation.

The ideas that you present will still need to win buy-in and must be on the hot-button list of your audience. By carefully doing the research for your high-stakes presentation, you will uncover the hot buttons and place them strategically in your talk. You should collect as much diverse information as possible so that it helps solve problems and provides new opportunities for your audience.[5]

Robert Cialdini, a leading persuasion theorist, wrote a classic best seller in 1984 titled *Influence* that highlighted six principles governing the science of persuasion: reciprocity, social proof, liking, consistency, authority, and scarcity. A high-stakes presentation in the age of speed would benefit from all six principles.

In 2016, Cialdini updated his classic book with new and significant information and titled it *Pre-Suasion*, making the argument that the window of time before an important message is most critical and determinative in the mind of the listener. He called this new concept "elevated attention," a step that is accomplished by redirecting the focus of attention before relevant action, in much the same way a magician might shift audience attention before the magic act is completed. He cites an experiment conducted by communication scientists San Bolkan and Peter Andersen that involved workers in a mall setting; they asked these individuals one question before conducting a survey: "Do you consider yourself a helpful person?" If the consumer answered yes, he or she was more likely to participate in the survey. With this tactic of elevated attention, participation rates jumped from 29 percent to 73.3 percent.[6] This form of "pre-suasion" can change the dynamic of the presentation and predispose your audience to accept your ideas.

Storytelling is the secret sauce of the high-stakes presentation, and I have devoted a full chapter to telling powerful stories. It makes sense that the high-stakes presenter who has the most authentic stories carries the day in the high-stakes presentation game. Just recall the success of Steve

Jobs in making his product presentations mostly about stories that we still remember and tell to other people.

Leaders set the tone and control the nature of the communications experience by telling stories that move people to action, and this is particularly true for the high-stakes presentation in the age of speed.

In short, storytelling is an important way to persuade your high-stakes audience. We all love stories, and we remember most vividly the stories our parents and grandparents told us when we were growing up. Forty or fifty years later, we can recall these stories from memory and retell them to our own children and friends. Yet often we cannot remember the movie we saw or the dinner we ate in the prior week. Clearly, the authentic stories we tell are embedded in our minds and carry a personal connection that resonates with us and stays with us forever. It is no wonder that Hollywood, Apple, and Disney rely so much on storytelling—it has become a mythical part of our culture.

Why has the professional and business world failed to take advantage of storytelling? I believe it is because we believe storytelling only works in Hollywood and has little relevance in our professional world. In recent years many CEOs have come to see that in the right context, stories resonate with customers, so much so that they will buy our products, humanize the organization, and elevate our reputation. Authentic storytelling will even help make us more trustworthy and more empathetic with highly influential decision makers. Stephen Covey, a leading management theorist, has preached this gospel for over twenty years in his books and speeches.

This book has fifteen chapters with a proprietary blueprint to help you fast-track your presentation. Part one helps you prepare your high-stakes presentation with the five **Laser Code** steps: **L**everaging your talk + **A**dapting to audience needs and analytics + **S**haring your ideas and achieving buy-in + **E**ducating stakeholders with powerful stories + **R**evealing novel approaches, innovative ideas, and solutions.

Part two helps you master the high-stakes presentation by effectively communicating your talk orally, visually, and kinesthetically. It has lessons and takeaways from *TED Talks* and *Shark Tank* presentations. It also explains how to use presentation technology and social media.

Part three is about delivering the high-stakes presentation with platform tips, staging advice, ways to finish strong, and making your ideas stick. It includes an important section on team dynamics as well as a section on becoming a question-and-answer pro and handling the media.

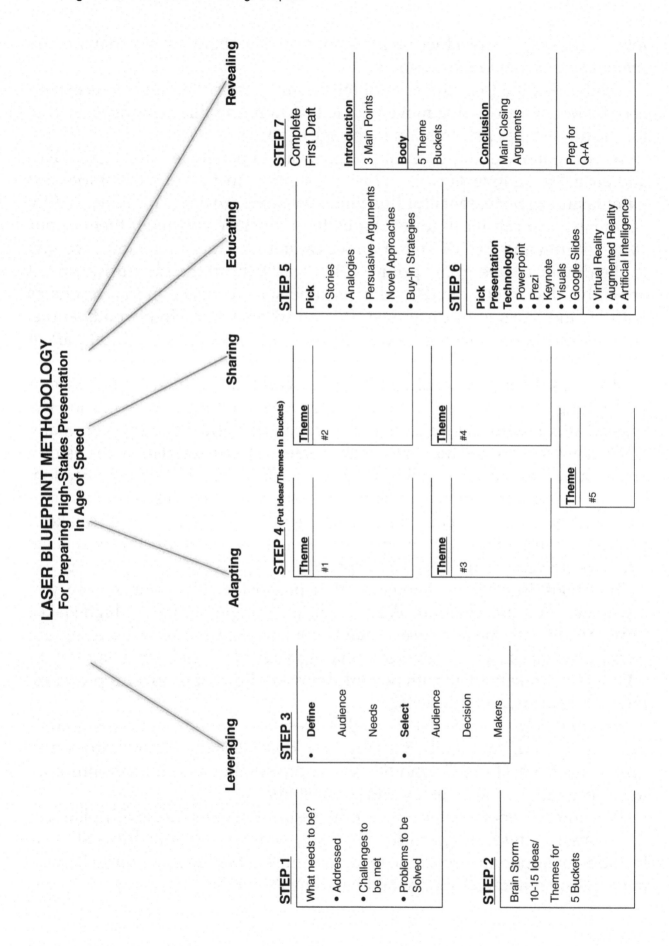

LASER BLUEPRINT METHODOLOGY
For Preparing High-Stakes Presentation
In Age of Speed

Leveraging   Adapting   Sharing   Educating   Revealing

STEP 1

What needs to be?

• Addressed

• Challenges to be met

• Problems to be Solved

STEP 2

Brain Storm

10-15 Ideas/
Themes for

5 Buckets

STEP 3

• **Define**
    Audience
    Needs

• **Select**
    Audience
    Decision
    Makers

STEP 4 (Put Ideas/Themes In Buckets)

Theme
#1

Theme
#2

Theme
#3

Theme
#4

Theme
#5

STEP 5

Pick
• Stories
• Analogies
• Persuasive Arguments
• Novel Approaches
• Buy-In Strategies

STEP 6

Pick
Presentation
Technology
• Powerpoint
• Prezi
• Keynote
• Visuals
• Google Slides

• Virtual Reality
• Augmented Reality
• Artificial Intelligence

STEP 7
Complete
First Draft

Introduction
3 Main Points

Body
5 Theme
Buckets

Conclusion
Main Closing
Arguments

Prep for
Q+A

Summary

1. Learn to harness speed with new digital tools in the age of speed.

2. Speeches, movies, and shows from more than a decade ago have a much slower pace than what is available today.

3. Persuasive messages have grown exponentially and are constantly changing on social media platforms. Need to be packaged with video, audio, and data.

4. The Laser code blueprint methodology and its five-step process provide a framework for high-stakes presentation.

5. Leaders are often the driving force for creating and presenting high-stakes presentations in the age of speed.

Exercises

1. Analyze famous speeches: The scripts of famous speeches past and present are available at Americanrhetoric.com and Youtube.com. Pick two speeches, one pre-1970 and one post-2015 and notice how the pace of the talk in the pre-1970 era is much slower, but picks up significantly in the post-2015 era talk. Speculate why this is so and write a short brief (about 150 words) to explain your answer.

2. Pick a topic on social media trends. Put together a short presentation outline of how you might organize this talk in the Age of Speed. It should include:

    A. Audience analysis

    B. Topic ideas (at least 3 to 5)

    C. Select open and closing remarks

    D. Suggest visuals

    E. Pick three persuasive messages for the talk

3. Describe five qualities from the list below that best describes the attributes of a high-stakes presenter in the age of speed.

    A. Curious

    B. Disciplined

    C. Reliable

    D. Tolerant

    E. Reliable

    F. Self-assured

    G. Trustworthy

Notes

1. Frank J. Pietrucha, *SuperCommunicator: Explaining the Complicated So Anyone Can Understand* (AMACOM, 2014), Chapter 5, Part 1, 7–9.

2. Ken McArthur, *Impact: How to Get Noticed, Motivate Millions and Make a Difference in a Noisy World* (Career Press, 2008), Chapter 1.

3. David Bartlett, *Making Your Point: Communicating Effectively with Audiences of One to One Million* (St. Martin's Press, 2008), 27–48.

4. Connie Dieken, *Talk Less, Say More: 3 Habits to Influence Others and Make Things Happen* (John Wiley & Sons, 2009), 29–34.

5. Norbert Aubuchon, *The Anatomy of Persuasion* (AMACOM, 1997), Introduction, 1–16.

6. Robert Cialdini, *Pre-Suasion: A Revolutionary Way to Influence and Persuade* (Simon & Schuster, 2016), Chapter 1, Chapter 2, 24–25.

PART 1

Preparing for High-Stakes Presentations

Leveraging Your High-Stakes Talk–Important Steps

2

> *"Leveraging Existing Resources is Innovation's sweetest play"*
>
> —RICHIE NORTON

Leveraging a high-stakes talk needs a short objective, plan of action, and context research, all-important elements to achieve a winning presentation. Many professional presenters often forget that "leverage" as the driving force that will help them with essential influencers who can advance or stop important proposals from going ahead.

After all, by having a strong objective, plan of action, and context research, you as a key presenter, will have more control over the persuasion process of the high-stakes presentation.

Let's take each element separately:

1. Objective: You must be able to write a brief objective of fifty words or less. If you can't do it, in fifty words or less, you are probably not ready to move forward with your high-stakes presentation.

   The longer you take to explain what you are trying to achieve, the more likely that you are not fully invested in your concept or proposal. What's more, it will not have the punch you will need to make your talk a success. John Kennedy's objective to go to the moon included 157 critical words in a speech at Rice Stadium in Houston, Texas on September 12, 1962. Let's look at the power and punch of those words:

   "But if I were to say, my fellow citizens, that we shall send to the moon, 240,000 miles away from the control station in Houston, a giant rocket more than 300 feet tall, the length of a football field, made of new metal alloys, some of which have not yet been invented, capable of standing heat and stresses several times more than have ever been experienced, fitted together with a precision better than the finest watch, carrying all the equipment needed for propulsion, guidance, control, communications,

© Luc Vernimmen/Shutterstock.com

food and survival, on an untried mission, to an unknown celestial body, and then return it safely to earth, re-entering the atmosphere at speeds of over 25,000 miles per hour, causing heat about half that of the temperature of the sun—almost as hot as it is here today—and do all this, and do it right, and do it first before this decade is out—then we must be bold.[1]

2. Plan of action: Your plan provides energy and momentum, giving your audience a blueprint for success. President Kennedy's plan of action for politicians, industry leaders, and public opinion luminaries presents the case of putting a man on the moon and bringing him safely back to Earth.

3. Context research: President Kennedy's famous speech to put a man on the moon was at Rice University in Houston, Texas, a city noted for space exploration. He picked the critical stakeholders to listen to the speech and the general media to spread the message across the country and around the world.

Kennedy was able to leverage his talk with the right message, the right audience, the right place, at the right time. No wonder NASA succeeded in putting a man on the moon, Astronaut Neil Armstrong on July 24, 1969.

A critical element of leverage in your talk is communicating your commitment to the audience. It can't be boring and bland. It must be in the vivid and robust language that shows the audience that you mean what you say.

The best chance of getting your message heard is how creatively you and your team commit to the organization's beliefs, values, and overall mission.

Remember: It's not about you. It's about the audience and the direction that moves them forward. You should put your commitment to the action plan mentioned earlier.

Once the client organization knows that you have made this commitment to their beliefs, values, and mission, the more likely it will give your presentation a fair hearing.

Kaset International has a "way it is" model to frame critical messages.

For example, in any situation between two people, there are three ways to frame a key message:

1. The way I see it
2. The way you see it
3. The way it is

The point here is that others may have a different frame of reference from your frame. This is okay. However, once the audience knows that you are framing the key message "The Way It Is," you start to build your ethos and authenticity as a high-stakes presenter.[2]

Asking good questions is another essential tool for leverage. Here are some examples:

How will the audience make their decision once I lay out the facts and present my action plan?

How will the key decision-makers at the presentation weigh in?

Will marketing and sales have the final say or will it be as is often the case the accountants in the organization?

Very often in nonprofit organizations, the executive director and the board of directors will have the final say. In government, including the military, a contracting officer and technical team will make the final selection.

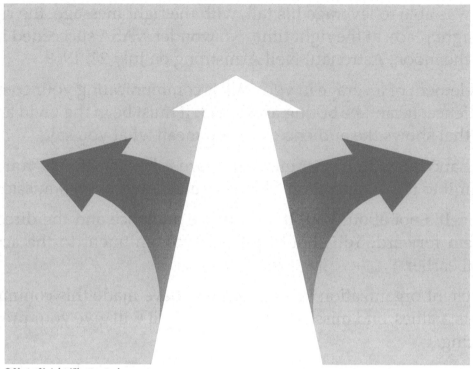

© VectorKnight/Shutterstock.com

Another step in leveraging your high-stakes presentation is the effective use of storyboarding to capture your key points and visuals. Many famous Hollywood producers, writers, and directors use this technique. Walt Disney is probably the most renowned film creator to use storyboarding at his studios in Disneyland. There he created Cinderella and Snow White and the Seven Dwarfs, among other famous films.

Today many high-stakes presenters use storyboarding to leverage their presentation with their influential audiences. The value of storyboarding for both famous film creators and high-stakes presenters is that it gives them a way to create a narrative story and make adjustments along the way. It is particularly true if you choose a PowerPoint template to create your high-stakes presentation. It provides a creative way to visualize your thoughts and put them in the order that is most imaginative and persuasive.

Putting your key idea messages in a story template will resonate more than a full bullet-point presentation and will not put your audience to sleep.

The storyboard will also provide a strong visual impact that many audiences crave in the digital age of speed. It combines visual and verbal messages. The visual ideas give the audience a picture of what will be seen during the presentation. You do not have to be an artist or graphic designer to make rough thumbnail sketches. Some high-stakes presenters use a whiteboard to illustrate their ideas. Others use more post-it notes that stick on the wall. Once the picture is created, it is much easier to add the spoken words for the presentation. In the age of speed, the visual message is the most powerful, and it's the best chance of being remembered by the audience.

You can plan your storyboard strategy in the slide sorter view in PowerPoint. It can also help with your plan for the high-stakes presentation. Cliff Atkinson, a leading authority on how to improve communications in organizations, recommends using storyboarding as a way to engage your audience with PowerPoint. Most of the times, your high-stakes presentation will be in a live environment with only a short time frame to get it right.

Atkinson recommends three ground rules for building a PowerPoint presentation:

1. Make your media transparent and slides simple to avoid being distracted by unnecessary details and design. Make the story structure invisible with the flow of the story.

2. Create a dialogue with your audience with engaging and interactive material.

3. Improvise with constraints. Think about how a jazz ensemble improvises with its audience. The ensemble has mastered the music fundamentals, but it allows for some play with the audience to bolster the connection. All three-ground rules will help you leverage your presentation.[3]

In planning the perfect high-stakes presentation, you will need to leverage the presentation by organizing particular pieces of information: your key messages, your visuals, your wow ideas, infographics, and story narratives. Much of this information will appear in the body of the speech, but some should be reserved for introduction and conclusion.

It is important to remember that information by itself will not produce a high-stakes presentation. It's how you transfer the information into a coherent narrative with an emotional component that will determine if the performance is a winner.

After all, high-stakes presenters are not surprised when told that a coherent narrative is the singlemost crucial part of their presentations. Powerful visuals can be very helpful and support the narrative, but they can't carry the presentation. It's all about the story, the story, the story, the most valuable real estate in a presentation.

Even a highly technical audience enjoys an excellent narrative presentation, and it helps boost the presenter's credibility with the influential audience. The integration of your material, nonvisual clues, and your empathy toward your audience is what ultimately gives you the leverage to slam-dunk your high-stakes presentation.

Joseph Sommerville in his book "Rainmaking Presentations: How to Grow Your Business by Leveraging Your Expertise" notes "a great novel contains many different parts such as plot, character development, and setting." In isolation, no individual piece can sustain the interest of a reader. Artful integration of the parts, however, creates a world of literature.

In a similar way, in the high-stakes presentation, the different aspects of integration with the audience including content, nonverbal signals, visuals, or audio connected will produce the best result.[4]

In planning your high-stakes presentation, it can be useful if you have a systematic plan to get the results you want. The laser blueprint in this book (Chapters 2, 3, 4, 5, and 6) provides a systematic approach to guide you along the way. It gives the high-stakes presenter a workable game plan to move the presentation smoothly along. Painting pictures and offering benefit statements will resonate with your audience and make it more authentic.

As in football, baseball, basketball, as well as the performance arts, nothing happens unless a plan is in place to shape the performance. The plan you develop should have a place for improvisation just in case you and your team run into "banana peels" that could derail your effort. The best high-stake presenters have a Plan B to adjust for unplanned factors. As any good speech coach will tell you, at the start of an important project, the blueprint is essential to make sure that you have your ducks in a row.

Another step that can provide you with leverage is the ability to use the power of inquiry to ask and find the right questions related to the needs of your high-stakes presentation. As an added benefit, the power of inquiry will help you find the elephant in the room, often called the hidden agenda, the situation that most likely will derail your presentation.

Frank Sesno, a former CNN anchor, White House correspondent, and Washington Bureau Chief, has written a book "Ask More: The Power to Open Doors,

Uncover Solutions, and Spark Change." He talks about strategic questions, diagnostic questions, creativity questions, mission questions, entertaining questions, among others.[5]

Sesno's types of questions that can help you prepare for your high-stakes presentations are:

Strategic:

1. What is the big picture here? Why does it matter?
2. What are we up against? Other competitors? Big issues in the workplace?
3. Do we have a plan that works?
4. Are there any holes in our plan?
5. What would success look like if we win?

Diagnostic Questions:

1. Why is this organization in so much trouble? Is it internal challenges?
2. Where do the problems originate?
3. What isn't working?
4. What are we not seeing?
5. What should we do?

Creativity Questions:

1. What is possible in this situation?
2. Consider this challenge from a different time, place, or perspective.
3. If we could start over, what would we do differently?
4. What new ideas, new concepts, could solve this challenge?
5. What would we do if we knew we could not fail?

Mission Questions:

1. What worries the organization the most?
2. What values shape this organization and its stakeholders?
3. What does this organization stand for?
4. What's needed to motivate the workforce?
5. How can we play a role in achieving the goal?

Besides good questions, the words, symbols, and images that you select for your talk can be tied to the overall vision. The vision is your guiding purpose for the talk that must resonate with your audience, and it must give them confidence that you can make it happen. The most effective high-stakes presentations move from information to influence to persuasion.

There is a quote from Chris Anderson from the TED Organization that appears in Ben and Kelly Decker's book, "Communicate to Influence: How to Inspire Your Audience to Action." This offers one of the best pieces of advice that I have found for high-stakes presenters. It states, "What would happen if you wanted to persuade a bunch of people to come along with you on a journey? What are the two things you need to do? Well, you got to start where they are, and you got to give them a reason to come along."[6]

There is no doubt in my mind if you follow Chris Anderson's advice, you are bound to make your high-stake presentation highly leverageable, easy to follow, and easy to remember.

A sure way to get the audience to come along is to fit the needs of the receivers. One of the best ways to gain leverage for your talk is to give them information the way they like to receive it. Some want the facts, although this is less and less common in the current culture.

Some want the big picture, a chance to see your macro view of the world. Some want a no-nonsense presentation with few frills. This type of performance is often associated with a highly technical audience. Some want a narrative presentation linked with a story or group of stories that carry the messages of your high-stakes presentation. Most likely, a combination of the big picture, facts, and human nature (story narrative) will give you the most leverage for your high-stakes presentation.

It's no wonder that today's politicians, luminaries, and business professionals provide a blend of the big picture, facts, and story to bring their messages to audiences in the age of speed.

Summary

1. Leveraging a high-stakes talk needs a short objective, plan of action, and context research.
2. Asking good diagnostic questions is another critical tool for leverage. Just layout the facts and an action plan.
3. The storyboard will provide a strong visual impact that many audiences crave in the digital age of speed.
4. In high-stakes presentations integrating content, non-verbal signals, visuals, and audio will produce the best results.
5. Politicians, luminaries, and business professionals often provide a blend of big ideas, facts, and story to bring their messages to audiences in the age of speed.

Exercises

1. Go to Goodreads.com and download John Kennedy's talk on going to the moon that was delivered at Rice University in Houston, Texas, September 12, 1962.

   a. In your view, what makes this talk important for its time and therefore a high-stakes presentation?
   b. How could Kennedy have used social media (not available in his time) to make his speech more prominent?

2. Explain the value of storyboarding for high-stakes presentations in the age of speed and how might you storyboard a short ten-minute presentation on the importance of social media for high-profile people, including celebrities and politicians.
3. Explain how you could use the art of questions (strategic, diagnostic, creative, and mission-related) to improve a high-stakes presentation about how the United Nations handles essential global issues.

Notes

1. https://er.jsc.nasa.gov/she/ricetalk.
2. Barbara Glanz; *The Great Communicator: 399 Tools to Communicate without Boring People to Death* (Homewood, IL: Kaset International, Business One Irwin, 1993).

3. Clint Atkinson, *Beyond Bullet Points: Using PowerPoint to Create Presentations That Inform, Motivate, and Inspire* (Microsoft Press, 2005), 182–87.

4. Joseph Sommerville, *Rainmaking Presentations: How to Grow Your Business by Leveraging Your Expertise* (Palgrave Macmillan, 2009), 68–69.

5. Frank Sesno, *Ask More: The Power of Questions to Open Doors, Uncover Solutions, and Spark Change* (AMACOM, 2017).

6. Ben Decker and Kelly Decker, *Communicate to Influence: How to Inspire Your Audience to Action* (McGraw-Hill, 2015), 141.

Adapting to Your Audience 3

"The best presenters have conversations with their audiences."

—ROBERT BLY

Adapting to your audience and getting insight into their needs is one of the best ways to gain support for your high-stakes presentation. This insight will give you the inside track to audience thinking and the direction they may want to move. It will also help shape your approach to the high-stakes presentation and strengthen its structure. Moreover, it will provide you with a road map to attract the attention of your audience, and help win them over.

For starters, you should start with finding out what the audience cares about, the challenges they face, and perhaps more importantly, "what is the elephant in the room" or the so-called hidden agenda.

Kevin Allen, an expert in business development and a former top executive for the McCann WorldGroup, has written a book "The Hidden Agenda." He argues that for people to follow you and embrace what you are selling is all about creating a connection that assures a mutual win. You should have a sense of the audience's fears (what keeps them up at night), their recent setbacks, and why they asked you and your team to pitch the organization.[1]

It would also help if you can define the issues that evoke the strongest emotions. Figure out how much detailed information is appropriate for the audience, and who is the best person/team in your organization to deliver the high-stakes presentation. Also, what are the hot topics to cover and avoid? The person/team that has the most robust connection with the audience will likely prevail when the competition is most rigorous.[2]

Most of all, you should become an audience advocate, one who serves their interests and needs. Many presenters make the critical mistake of creating a high-stakes presentation to serve their needs while giving less attention to the audience's needs. Ideally, you want your audience to trust that you will act on their behalf.

Furthermore, you must provide them with a reason or series of ideas to work on your behalf. They will act on your behalf only when their interests are supported by your stated intentions.

Your audience is looking for your ethos (credibility), logos (the logic of your argument), and pathos (the passion you bring to the assignment); it also needs to see the visual reinforcement of your message and the journey you are taking them on from A to B to C.

Visual reinforcement is so important because it is the mode of learning that is most prevalent in society, schools, and institutions. It is no secret that we are becoming more and more a visual society as the "screen," whether in our devices or digital TV, has become more prominent. Visual effects, whether in movies, plays, or at the entertainment parks, still dazzle us no matter how old we are. The old masters from Walt Disney to Steve Jobs understood the power of the visual and demonstration and used them with great effect. Benjamin Franklin was famous for this quote, "Tell me, and I forget; teach me and I may remember; involve me and I learn."

Your high-stakes presentation needs to involve your audience in three ways:

1. Make the story in your presentation about them.
2. Give them some "skin in the game," so the investment makes sense to them.
3. Share ideas that solve their problems, offer them a solution, and give them a competitive edge on breakthroughs.

The story is the focal point that can drive the narrative and help them remember your presentation.

Skin in the game makes them a vested partner with you and a more likely client to stay the course with you.

The sharing of breakthrough ideas and solutions to their problems and challenges convinces them that you and your creative team can help them achieve their goals.

Alan Alda of the TV show "MASH" fame and a great communicator in his own right, has written a new book on effective communication titled "If I Understood You, Would I Have This Look on My Face: My Adventures in the Art and Science of Relating and Communicating." He noted that two factors, more than others, will help get your message across.

1. Theory of mind: Getting inside the heads and minds of your audience so that you learn where they are coming from.

2. Empathy: Having the ability to walk in their shoes and understand how they feel about what you are trying to convince/persuade them to do.[3]

From Alda's experiences in TV and on Broadway, he understands full well that people won't come along with you unless they know you care about them.

Assessing your high-stakes audience will play a significant role in the success of your presentation. Many presenters often fail to understand who their audience is. In short, they don't do their homework and instead rely on a limited number of people to make judgments about the audience.

Here are some criteria you can use to learn more about your audience:

1. Is it a specific group or a general audience? A management or leadership audience has high-level executives and decision-makers from industry, nonprofit organizations, or government. They want the big picture and solutions to their problems. Most, if not all, high-stakes presentations are associated with a leadership audience.

2. Why are they attending? Are they invited or guests? What are they looking for—industry information, advances in technology, policy initiatives?

3. What is their level of knowledge about your topic? Basic or advanced?

4. Will cultural factors play a role in the presentation? International audience? Culturally diverse?

5. What are the demographic breakdowns? Young managers, middle managers, or a little of both groups?

High-stakes audiences most likely will be interested in current events that impact them. Be up-to-date on what events will resonate positively with them. Besides, if you can find geographic connections or local tie-ins that relate to what your audience likes and that can make a difference. Finally, the content of your presentation should be relevant to your audience's industry or business.[4]

The ideal high-stakes presentation should be shared by fifty or fewer people. It certainly can be given to larger audiences and achieve optimal results. The small audience, however, may be open to a more nuanced argument and produce more unity for compliance with your ideas.

Positive group behavior can lead the audience to support the high-stakes presenter if the core messages are linked to collective hopes and fears that the audience shares with the presenting organization. It is especially true of high-stakes political speeches that are aimed at large audiences of two hundred or more people.

Nevertheless, the high-stakes presenter must always remember that he or she is most likely trying to influence and gain the support of a small number of people who can shape the destiny of the organization.

While some experts may disagree with the following advice, you must invite the audience to participate at every stage of the presentation, and not just at the end. It will show them that you have the confidence (ethos) to handle the presentation and that you are credible.

The tone of your presentation must be a conversational dialogue, open, and never scripted.

Another way to adapt to your audience is to figure out the probable disposition of the group. Are they likely to be supportive, hostile, or neutral group? More than likely, the person who will introduce you will give you some clues related to the disposition of the audience participants.

You must think like a chess master, staying ahead of your opponent and predicting his or her moves down the road.

The reputation or the prestige of the person who will introduce you should provide some insight about what you can expect and, to some extent, a clue as to how you will be received. Try and get the highest-level person in the group or organization to introduce you to the audience.

© Nosyrevy/Shutterstock.com

Very often, audience types will vary, some with dominant personalities and traits. Here are some examples:

1. Analytical thinker: Most times, these are individuals from accounting, engineering, computer science, and systems analysis who want to know how you justify and quantify the conclusions of your presentation.

2. Relater/Feeler: These individuals typically share a social conscience and nurturing personality who want to know that your conclusions will make the organization feel warm, safe, and happy. Statistics will not be as important as good visuals and an active emotional component.

3. Leaders and Managers: This audience typically wants the "big picture" and information that will move the mission along and produce good results. With this audience, don't spend a lot of time diagramming the process; get to the point, and have an actionable case.

4. Expressives: This type watches how you talk and perform. They may be associated with performance-related jobs in sales and marketing, and want to see the high-stakes presenter dazzle the audience and present something new and novel.

Very often, sending your intended audience a preprogram speech questionnaire can help you and your team discover the hidden agenda as well as the movers and shakers planning to attend your presentation.

Ray Anthony, a top speaking consultant, has written an inspirational book, "Talking to the Top: Executive's Guide to Career Making Presentations." He suggests essential ways to analyze and find out about your audience. They include:

1. What do they know about your talk? What is their experience with it and has it been covered before?

2. What are their attitudes and opinions? Anthony suggests knowing where they stand emotionally and intellectually will help you design

the content of your talk and your persuasive strategy. Equally important would be how can they benefit or be hurt by what you are proposing.

3. What are their needs, desires, and expectations? In this case, according to Anthony, they could want to see the specific financial and market-related information. You need to know what the audience must know to decide on your idea and proposal under consideration.

4. What are their priorities and "pain points"? Anthony points out that if the presenter can focus on the priorities and reduce the level of pain, the audience will listen and is more likely to respond favorably to your proposal. Anthony suggests that you should know what sensitive issues should and should not be left out.

5. What are their mood and conditions? Anthony wants the speaker to understand the emotional, mental, and physical state of the audience. The way they feel can dramatically impact the reception of the message. Try to schedule your talk at the time of day when they will be fresh and ready to hear and respond to your talk. If the mood is upbeat, find a way to use the mood to help you reach the goals of your talk. Also, according to Anthony, you should have a Plan B if the audience is restless and under pressure at work.

6. How many will be there? A small audience is easy to relate to and engage with. A large audience is more apt to sit back with a "show me" attitude. Audience size, according to Anthony, will dictate the visual aids you decide to use.

7. What are their positions and professions? Anthony points out that the make-up of your audience, mostly technical or mostly sales and marketing, will determine your content and the way you relate to your audience. Marketing and Salespeople prefer the "big picture" instead of a detailed analysis of each point, as Anthony shares in his book.

8. What are their professional backgrounds? Anthony notes that by finding out about their personal backgrounds, it will lead you to their values, beliefs, and attitudes. Here is the list that Anthony shares in his book:

    i. What types of people generally impress the audience?

    ii. Who are their heroes or heroines?

    iii. What achievements were audience members particularly proud of?

    iv. Are they formal or informal types of people?

    v. Conservative or liberal?

   vi. What degree of risk-takers are they? None? Very cautious? Prudent? High?

  vii. How do they view innovation and creativity?

 viii. What is their leadership style?

   ix. What do they fear or worry about?

    x. What drives them and turns them on?

   xi. How might your audience members describe themselves?

  xii. What clubs, associations, or groups do they belong to that would give you a clue as to who they are?

9. How do they make decisions?

    i. Who sways the group?

   ii. Who makes the decisions?

  iii. What type of information would they need to make a decision?

  iv. What criteria, such as financial payback, technology, or market experience, has the most weight and why?

   v. What emotional appeals would work the best?

  vi. How would they perceive risk related to your proposal? [5]

Summary

1. Presenters need to find the "elephant in the room" or so-called hidden agenda for their high-stakes presentation as well the challenges they face and where they came from.

2. Your audience is looking for the ethos (credibility), logos (logic), and pathos (passion) you bring to the assignment.

3. Sharing the breakthrough ideas and solutions to their problems and challenges convinces the audience that you can help them achieve their goals.

4. Alan Alda's theory of the mind (getting inside the heads and minds of your audience) and empathy (having the ability to walk in their shoes) will play a significant role in the success of your presentation.

5. Know the disposition of the audience from the analytical thinker, the relater-feeler, leaders and managers, or expressives to help you and your team succeed.

Exercises

1. How would you apply audience analysis tools included in this chapter for a talk on how young people in their twenties and thirties spend their disposable time on their tablets and watching TV and other special services such as Netflix and Hulu?

2. Explain how audience types such as analytical thinker, relater-feeler, leaders/managers, and expressives might critique a speech "On Spending Habits of College-Educated Consumers."

3. What insights on public speaking does the famous actor of the MASH TV series and PBS Science Shows offer to public speakers making talks in their professional field of work?

Notes

1. Kevin Allen, *The Hidden Agenda: A Proven Way to Win Business and Create a Following* (Bibliomotion, 2012), 67–70.

2. Frank J. Pietrucha, *Super Communicator: Explaining the Complicated So Any One Can Understand* (New York: AMACOM, 2014).

3. Alan Alda, *If I Understood You, Would I Have This Look on My Face* (New York: Random House, 2017).

4. Rhonda Abrams, *Winning Presentation in a Day* (Palo Alto, California: The Planning Shop, 2005), 11–12, 27–29.

5. Ray Anthony, *Talking to the Top: Executive's Guide to the Top Career Making Presentations* (New York: Prentice-Hall, 1995), 34–44.

Sharing Your Ideas and Achieving Buy-In 4

"Some people want it to happen, some wish it would happen, and others make it happen."

—MICHAEL JORDAN

Effectively sharing your ideas starts with planning the presentation with a precise and limited objective that could be placed on the back of a business card or in a 140-character tweet. Another equally important goal is to make sure you leave a final impression that your audience will remember, preferably by concluding your presentation with an important takeaway. A strong beginning and ending is critical in the age of speed because our focus as professionals has taken a hit with the overflow of information from the Internet and social media. You must also establish a strong connection with your audience, moving your audience closer to a commitment and consensus that makes acceptance of your big ideas or proposal possible.

The most useful aspect of your high-stakes presentation may be the selection and placement of your novel approaches, ideas, and solutions for your influential decision makers. If done correctly, the audience will start mentally applying these solutions to achieve their overall goals. After all, the chief objective of the high-stakes presenter is to make ideas easy to understand by introducing a narrative arc that resonates with the audience from both a logical and emotional perspective.

The high-stakes presenter needs to establish what the audience needs to know, care about, and act on. What many high-stakes presenters fail to do is to meet audience expectations, primarily because they are caught up in meeting their own needs. Bill Bernbach, the legendary advertising executive said, "You can say the right thing about a product and nobody will listen. You got to say it in such a way people would feel it in their gut. Because if they don't feel it, nothing will happen."[1]

In his book *Presentations That Change Minds: Strategies to Persuade, Convince, and Get Results*, Josh Gordon cites one of the most powerful high-stakes presentations on civil rights in the twentieth century. Most remember it as the "I Have a Dream" speech by Dr. Martin Luther King. What many do not remember is that it lasted less than sixteen minutes and became critical in the passage of the civil rights bill. Yet the bill was not mentioned in the speech, and no statistics or formal proofs were offered. It was persuasion by emotional appeal along with the high credibility of the speaker that made it work.[2]

Now this is not to take anything away from logical analysis or the use of statistics in high-stakes presentations. It just so happens that an appeal to our visual nature and pure emotion often carries the day. Many professionals somehow believe that business executives or high-level professionals want just the facts. Yet often they are proven wrong because what influential decision makers remember and retain is the gist of a powerful strategic story that makes the case for their organizations. The facts, unless they are dramatic or have an emotional component, remain difficult to remember and retain.

To test your emotional variance, try to sense the feelings you have for the following list of items:

1. Your experiences and good times with friends and colleagues at college or grad school
2. The best advice you received from your high school teacher, coach, or college professor
3. Life experiences growing up in your hometown
4. Your first professional job
5. Your first boyfriend, girlfriend, or partner

Now take a look at this list and record your feelings:

1. Pepsi or Coke

2. BMW

3. Apple

4. Amazon

Most likely, your emotions jumped when you looked at the first list and were much more subdued when you looked at the second list (unless, of course, you had the fortunate opportunity to drive a Z3 BMW, as I have for the past fifteen years). The second list of brands is backed by millions of dollars of promotion to get your emotional attachment. Yet with all their spending, it is the first list that strikes a chord with you because the story is more authentic to you and resonates with your heart and not your head. Emotions are very much an important part of the audience's decision-making process. This is even more so in the age of speed because professionals are pushed to make quicker decisions and to come to definitive conclusions on important business matters.

Because people learn information in different ways, the sharing of ideas must appeal to the eyes for visual learners, resonate to the ears for the auditory audience, and provide hands-on activities for those who want a kinesthetic mode.

Learning Styles

VISUAL	AUDITORY
KINESTHETIC	MULTIMODE

Naturally, a high-stakes presenter who connects to all our learning styles will be more successful with influential decision makers. Unfortunately, the reason many presenters never make an impression on the audience is because they fail to connect visually with the audience and rely solely on bullet points in a PowerPoint presentation, allowing most of the audience to tune out very quickly.

Another way to help the speaker cement audience interest is to find converts and allies. These champions and cheerleaders for your cause and big ideas can help you over tough spots in the presentation and provide the momentum you need when it matters the most. In an effort to win converts and allies, Samuel Bacharach, a negotiation expert and head of Cornell University's Institute of Workplace Studies, suggests that having political competence is most helpful and essential. He notes, "Political competence is the ability to understand what you can and cannot control, when to take action, anticipate who is going to resist your agenda and determine whom you need on your side to push your agenda."[3]

Political competence may be the most critical skill a high-stakes presenter can bring to the presentation game. Most failed high-stakes presentations arguably do not take into consideration the political agenda in the planning process leading up to the big presentation. The skilled high-stakes presenter knows that having political competence is necessary to achieve buy-in. One aspect of political competence is having empathy, being aware of the interests of others and moving the agenda forward in spite of the obstacles. You will need to be fully aware of how to understand and analyze the dynamics of the upcoming presentation environment.

Although converts and allies can help push your agenda, resisters can lay the groundwork to derail it. The resistance can be low key so as to hold your ideas hostage. These audience members can resist your ideas so they no longer resemble their original form. Or, in the worst-case scenario, the resisters will work to eliminate your ideas and take them off the table.

To achieve buy-in, you must prepare for some resistance and be able to understand the mindsets of the people in the organization or client team. Many of the resisters may have goals and perspectives that are different from what you present. You will need to know whether you can reconcile the differences and viewpoints so that you can better make your case by adjusting the arc of the narrative with a stronger argument and more emotional component.

Bacharach makes it clear that in getting buy-in, "your challenge is to persuade resisters and political allies that their support for your effort is beneficial to them."[4] This process may include having to adjust your agenda and presentation to address the concerns of the resisters and shore up support for the views of your allies.

Diagram of Allies and Resisters

Box 1. Full Support of Allies	Box 2. High- Level Resistance
Box 3. Marginal Support of Allies	Box 4. Marginal Support of Resisters

To move marginal support of allies (Box 3) and marginal support of resisters (Box 4) to your side, you need to do the following things:

1. Find their hidden agenda (Chapter 3).
2. Revise your narrative arc (Story and Agenda).
3. Bolster your credibility and show you can make it happen.
4. Form a new coalition.

By forming a new coalition (a group of supporters that share and support your ideas), you change the dynamics related to your high-stakes presentation and offer a new course of action. Winning over the resisters may not be doable, and you will just have to prepare for the new coalition to help you carry the day.

To further build support for your ideas in the high-stakes presentation, you will need to develop a relationship, tactical, and communications strategy.

A relationship strategy should include the following:

- Building trust. This aspect is fundamental to getting your ideas accepted in a timely manner.

- Creating a connection with your audience. This strategy makes the audience want to support and help you along.

- Understanding the emotions in the room. They can break a presentation, particularly when they are negative. Try to keep the stakeholders neutral and positive so they can be in position to accept your ideas.

- Showing empathy with the audience with enhanced listening skills. By listening carefully to comments during the presentation, you can pick up clues on where the presentation needs to go.

- Bonding with members of the stakeholder organization. The bond you create just before, during, and after the presentation will determine the extent of your success in closing the deal.

For a **tactical strategy**, the following steps are recommended:

- Reserve presentation time in the question-and-answer session for skeptics. Doing this will allow them to voice their concerns and you to handle a rebuttal as needed.

- Anticipate rebuttal topics from resisters and include these matters in your presentation so they have less chance of being brought up in the question-and-answer time.

- Include how you will accomplish your ideas and/or solutions as well as how you will measure the results along the way.

- Highlight any preliminary evidence that your proposal will work.

- Show a strong stage presence and confidence when presenting your ideas to key influential decision makers.

In a **communications strategy**, you should follow these guidelines:

- Keep the presentation highly visual and interactive as much as possible. In the age of speed, visuals matter more than words and have a better chance of success with retention.

- Formulate a narrative arc with at least three main ideas. Our brains have been wired to the rule of three at home, at business, and at play. For example, past, present, and future (story narrative plot); lights, camera, action (Hollywood); reading, writing, and arithmetic (school); body, mind, spirit (health).

- Use success stories, metaphors, and anecdotes to support key messages and videos as necessary.

- Repeat core messages at least three times during the presentation for better retention.

- Always stay on message and keep focused on the movers and shakers in the room.

Mark Walton, a former chief White House correspondent for CNN, penned a book *Generating Buy-In: Mastering the Language of Leadership,* explaining how great leaders paint a big picture that generates action to accomplish goals. He draws on his experience as a top-tier journalist who has witnessed high-stakes

interviews and presentations during his career. He suggests developing your storyline in three chapters (the value of three again) that target your audience's particular needs, wants, and goals.

As one example, he uses Ronald Reagan's successful 1980 "Morning in America" campaign story that was built around targeted voter needs, wants, and goals. The three chapters that Reagan promised said that he would cut taxes and spur economic growth, strengthen America's military, and reduce the size of government.

By keeping his ideas simple and straightforward so that most Americans could understand them, Reagan's three key messages helped him win the White House, a stunning example of how a high-stakes presentation works in the political arena.[5]

It is no surprise that this simple and straightforward approach works in the business world as well. GE's popular ad campaign "We bring good things to life" under Jack Welch and cited by Walton helped the company recruit top talent and bolstered its reputation among business leaders and consumers.

In every high-stakes presentation, five principles help ensure that sharing ideas and achieving buy-in becomes possible:

1. Make ideas boldly new or a significant improvement of what came before.

2. Find an advocate in the organization that wants your ideas to succeed.

3. Make allies both inside and outside the organization where you are presenting your proposal.

4. Limit the role of resisters.

5. Avoid the organizational swamp where good ideas come to an end by the naysayers whose primary slogan is "been there, done that, and it didn't work."

It is important to remember that the high-stakes presentation is about seeing possibilities where none existed before. It is about sharing ideas and achieving buy-in for the most creative and adaptable ideas you and your team can present. After all, the high-stakes presenter must have the mindset of the innovator and the rhetorical skills to make people take action in the age of speed.

Albert Einstein said that "imagination is more important than knowledge." Even though he understood the importance of logic and knowledge, he was fascinated with imagination because he knew that is where breakthrough thinking emerges and takes hold in our mind.

When Steve Jobs gave his famous high-stakes presentation for the first iPhone, he must have known that his customers would see for themselves that a cell phone with a media player, calendar, camera, and text device would be bundled together in a sensational once-in-a-lifetime product. He took the roles of an innovator, businessman, and showman and made people around the world take notice in one of the most memorable high-stakes demonstrations in history. Of course, we cannot all be Steve Jobs or even reach his lofty status, but we can learn from him and others like him the critical elements of high-stakes presentations, and we can put those elements in our next presentation. In sum, we need to provide breakthrough thinking on our topic so that the high-stakes presentation resonates with influential decision makers.

Summary

1. Having a strong beginning and ending for your talk is critical in age of speed. It helps solidify your most important messages for buy-in.

2. Introduce a narrative arc in your talk that resonates with audience from both a logical and emotional perspective.

3. Emotions are a very important part of the audience's decision-making process and influence buy-in.

4. Skilled high-stakes presenters know that having political competence is necessary to achieve buy-in. Understand your allies and resisters.

5. To build support for your ideas in a high-stakes presentation, you will need to develop a relationship strategy, a tactical strategy, and a communications strategy.

Exercises

1. Analog/20th Century/Digital Approaches 21st Century. Put yourself in the analog age of public speaking and its approach to the audience. Then try to look at the world from the new digital age of speed and ask what the analog age of speaking did not have with regard to: technologies, social media platforms, visual representation, search engines, and audience feedback. Explain why in your opinion the digital presentation age of speed is more audience focused than the analog age of speaking.

2. How would you build support for a high-stakes presentation by arguing for more e-commerce/digital tools for retail " Big Box" stores to ensure their survival. Prepare relationship, tactical, and communications approaches for this task.

3. Conduct research online and at your library. Report on the presentation secrets of Steve Job, the former CEO of Apple. What did he do to achieve buy-in with his audiences and stakeholders?

Notes

1. Josh Gordon, *Presentations That Change Minds: Strategies to Persuade, Convince and Get Results* (New York: McGraw Hill, 2006), 69.

2. Gordon, *Presentations That Change Minds*, 70.

3. Samuel B. Bacharach, *Get Them on Your Side* (Platinum Press, 2005), xviii.

4. Bacharach, *Get Them on Your Side*, 152.

5. Marc S. Walton, *Generating Buy-In: Mastering the Language of Leadership* (AMACOM, 2004), 31–37.

Why Educating Audiences with Powerful Stories Matters

"Storytelling is the most powerful way to put ideas into the world."

—Robert McKee

In *Business Storytelling for Dummies*, Karen Dietz and Lori Silverman illustrate how stories impact people in four ways. Number one is physical. Executives will sit up and listen if a story is relevant to their bottom line or business prospects. They will shift their physical behavior. They will stop taking notes and put down their electronic devices.

The second point is mental. Researchers at Princeton University have shown that, on average, the listener's brain response to a story links with that of the speaker's brain response, albeit with time delays that match the flow of the information.

The third point is emotional. Behavioral scientists note that the emotional brain is where trust, loyalty, and hope are activated and where unconscious, emotional decisions are formed.

The fourth point is the human spirit. Stories impact us as individuals if they touch the human spirit. Think back to accounts in your own life that were unforgettable, and you can probably trace those stories to significant events or upheavals that gave you a new perspective or ignited a transformative life change.[1]

Great stories work in television advertising too, whether in thirty–or sixty-second increments. Mastercard does it with style in its "priceless" commercials that many people remember: "A father and son at a

baseball game—two tickets, $28; two hotdogs, two popcorns, and two sodas, $18. One autographed baseball: Priceless."[2] People love stories with emotional appeal, especially if those stories are about America's favorite pastime.

The storytelling model can work in a high-stakes presentation when delivered with passion, emotion, and a memorable tagline. It is important to remember that logic will take you only so far in a high-stakes presentation. You will need a good story to bring you all the way.

One of the most potent storytellers in American history was Walt Disney, the animator, film producer, and entrepreneur. His achievements include all the great movies he produced, such as *Snow White and the Seven Dwarfs* in 1937, *Pinocchio* in 1940, *Dumbo* in 1941, *Bambi* in 1942, *Cinderella* in 1950, and *Mary Poppins* in 1964.

All those movies became classics, and if they were shown in movie theaters today, they would still be spellbinding for young and old alike. Disney knew how to tell a story, how to involve an audience emotionally, and how to make everyone feel good in the end.

Those three ingredients are necessary for a successful high-stakes presentation as well. Tell your story, involve your audience emotionally, and make everyone feel good at the end. Disney applied that three-step formula to his amusement parks in California and Florida and, today, millions of patrons from around the world make the trek to those locations and take home great memories.

The famous *Mickey Mouse Club* TV show also followed the three-step formula and became must-see for young people during its run from 1955 to 1996. Disney's storytelling transformed American society and made the Disney amusement park slogan, "The Happiest Place on Earth," come true for millions. And if you follow that Disney example by including a compelling story in your high-stakes presentation, it's more than likely your story will resonate with the audience because the storytelling plays such a significant role in American culture and cultures around the world.

The impact of stories makes them one of the most powerful tools to communicate your message to high-stakes audiences. Stories linked directly to your audience are usually much more effective than an array of statistics. If I gave you statistics on animal abuse in America, you would take notice. But if I showed you a picture of an abused dog or told you a story about the dog being abused and included video details, it would be more likely to move you to action or to open your wallet for a donation. The reason for our reaction is that we cannot feel data, but we can feel empathy for dogs as friends and family members.

Dr. Paul Zak, author, professor of economics in psychology and management, and director of the Center for Neuroeconomics Studies at Claremont Graduate School, has shown in his work that character-driven stories with emotional content result in a clearer understanding of the key points and enable a better read.[3]

Our society has been story-ready from our ancestors to digital media. Emotional stories can significantly and immediately change attitudes, opinions, and beliefs and sometimes can continue to influence these factors later, when the story takes on a different meaning. Is storytelling still relevant to the digital age? The short answer is yes, of course it is, because consumers value stories for the interpretations and perspectives they can provide.

You can no longer demand an audience's attention; you must earn it through storytelling. Kevin Allen notes that the classic story structure is the hero's journey that features a quest marked by many challenges. There is a reversal of

© Sammby/Shutterstock.com

fortune, when it looks like the hero may fail. Then there is the turning point, when the hero regains momentum. Finally, the eureka moment arrives when the hero wins the day, and all is well.[4]

If we present the hero's journey in a high-stakes presentation, we are likely to rally the audience to our side. Always consider the moral of the story and whether it connects with the challenge the audience faces. Storytelling is powerful when it includes the following four elements: (1) it makes us feel good and usually has a happy ending; (2) it often says that life can be better than it is now, so stick with it; (3) it includes obstacles and setbacks that must be overcome; and (4) the hero makes it home safely.

In a business context, substitute the company for the hero and feature business challenges for the obstacles and setbacks. Show the high-end mission and goals the company can achieve.

Finally, Allen identified these seven essential elements of the business story: (1) What opposing forces or villains do you face? (2) What is your core strategy at this point? (3) What is your quest, your real ambition? (4) Who are your heroes, and who are the heroes for the audience? (5) Will values and beliefs sustain your journey? (6) What is at stake; what is the hidden agenda at this particular point? (7) How will the story be resolved, and what does the future hold?[5]

Everything I have observed with executives shows that telling a story boosts the value of a high-stakes presentation in most business settings. That is true because business audiences usually are given fact-driven, statistical presentations and base-level performances that seem to go nowhere. They want the central idea of a presentation, and the story, most of the time, fits the bill.

A good story often introduces the subject of your presentation, but some presentations use inspirational stories for their own sake. They use the lives of historical people, businesspeople, or luminaries to introduce or discuss the story or journey. I know it sounds simple, and you may not believe storytelling will work for you, but top speech coaches have shown that a story elicits strong emotions that can be used to fortify high-stakes presentations.

Peter Guber, studio chief of Columbia Pictures, and other top executives in the entertainment industry say that aiming for the head and wallet can be counterproductive in high-stakes presentations. He cites a failed business venture with the mayor of Las Vegas that helped him realize that it was the heart, not the head, that we must work on to convince an audience. So, you weaken your chances of being heard if you fail to reach the heart of your audience.

In his book *Tell to Win*, Guber notes his mistake in Las Vegas and how he has used that experience to build a successful career. He learned that high-stakes presentations need to articulate a vision for the audience along with a pathway to achieve it. Effective high-stakes presenters know that digital media tools must give the audience a more immersive experience when it comes to storytelling. One way to ensure that experience is by using audio to draw on the voices of people or employees who have told their story to you. Those voices will make your account more authentic.[6]

Sometimes, showing high-impact images related to the story can make the chronology of the events come alive. Such images can help you sequence the story in your presentation. Showing a video will take the audience beyond the words and keep them engaged. It has become clear to high-stakes presenters that storytelling is not just for the Hollywood crowd.

Major companies and government agencies are expanding the use of storytelling and helping marketing and training executives learn how to do it well. Warren Buffett even uses stories in his letters to shareholders.

Ronald Reagan used storytelling in his famous Morning in America campaign in 1984 that helped him win the presidency. Barack Obama also used storytelling to make his case with the American people when he ran for president and also used it in his State of the Union Addresses.

Famous authors, including the late Stephen Covey and Spencer Johnson, feature stories to help bring their work to business audiences. A story in a business setting can refocus the marketing—and even the financial goals—of an organization.

A story about a nonprofit organization can jump-start the cause that improves the condition of people. A story told in a government agency can rally its workers to a new challenge, such as eradicating poverty. Stories, after a while, help audiences understand and process complex information. The litmus test for high-stakes presenters is how well they move the audience on a designated journey to the ultimate solution.

Summary

1. Most of the successful TED speakers use stories for maximum impact.
2. Aristotle's formula for persuasion (ethos, logos, and pathos) is essential for storytelling.
3. The world's best speakers from Toastmasters International rely on stories to deliver their magic at its International Speech Contest.
4. Neuroscience researchers are now pointing to the power of stories to help anchor ideas and improve the brain's processing of information.
5. Stories are becoming the perfect format in many media platforms, including social media.

Exercises

1. Listen and explain the four points of how stories impact people, as noted in the text by Karen Dietz and Lori Silverman.
2. Explain how the power of stories can be used in a high-stakes presentation.
3. Why can a story-based presentation by organizational leaders be more effective than a fact-driven, statistical presentation?

Notes

1. Karen Dietz and Lori Silverman, *Business Storytelling for Dummies* (John Wiley & Sons, 2013), 14–15.
2. Kevin Allen, *The Hidden Agenda* (Bibliomotion, 2012), 182–84.
3. Drew Turney, BrainWorld, Summer 2018, Emotion, Issue 4. Volume 9, pp 16–17.
4. Kevin Allen, *The Hidden Agenda* (Bibliomotion, 2012), 188–89.
5. Kevin Allen, *The Hidden Agenda*, 2012, p 201.
6. Peter Guber, *Tell to Win: Connect, Persuade and Triumph with the Hidden Power of Story* (Profile Books, 2011), 3–8.

Revealing Novel Approaches, Innovative Ideas, and Solutions

6

"Innovation is the calling card of the future."

—ANNA ESHOO

High-stakes presenters make a significant impression on the audience when they reveal an innovative approach or powerful solution the audience is not expecting and that becomes a game changer.

This innovative approach creates an important connection, a connection that solidifies the theme and main ideas outlined in the presentation. It also shows that the high-stakes presenter has the confidence to deliver his or her promises and that these ideas will help the organization accomplish its goals.

The novelty of the solution is important because it needs to stand out from the me-too solutions often offered in standard presentations that could not survive in a high-stakes presentation. Just like the powerful finale of a movie or play, the solution offered must make the audience feel that it is not the one they thought of, and it should be brilliant in its form and execution.

The novelty offered by the high-stakes presenter highlights the creative capacity needed to help the organization move forward on its path to a brighter future, one that has real promise for their stakeholders.

I cannot emphasize enough that the reveal of a novel approach, innovation, or idea must have some drama and come with a sense of enthusiasm that the client recognizes immediately. When offering a novel solution, you should make sure it builds on the working relationship with the client.[1] Also, you should ensure that the individual or team has the expertise to make the solution work and that the client trusts that you and your team will follow through.

Before the actual high-stakes presentation, the presenter needs to get the client to tell the team what problems they want solved. You must send your best team to the pre-meeting so the team can find out from the management team what is working and what is not. Often, the client can help define a communication problem, a technical issue, a revenue issue, or a tough competitive challenge.

Sometimes it is best for the high-stakes presenter to give the organization multiple options instead of just one single solution. A single solution takes a lot of firepower and may fail to get their final approval. Offering multiple solutions allows them to pick and choose the most formidable option for their needs. Of course, you need to let them know how you arrived at the multiple solutions and why you are confident they will work. If you and your team must go with a single solution, make sure it has multiple dimensions that demonstrate the wide range of thinking your team has done on the matter.

The offer of your persuasive solution should come only after you are confident that you have laid the groundwork with a powerful opening, a well-sequenced theme/argument, and the rationale to explain why it is tailored to meet the challenges the organization is facing.

It is important to remember that the high-stakes audience wants to know that you and your team bring insights and analysis that have relevance for their challenge/problem.

To arrive at novel approaches, innovations, and ideas, you need to access creative tools and applications to help make your solution a winning one. Here are ten approaches that will bolster your ability to find the most powerful solutions for your high-stakes presentation:

1. Brainstorming/mind mapping

Thinking on paper with a mind map is the fastest way to generate ideas for your high-stakes presentation. A mind map (see post-it notes visual representation) is a visual representation of your ideas that can be easily presented and easily understood by the audience without much confusion. This process allows you and your team to double or triple the output of your ideas; it is much faster than just a linear listing of ideas on paper or in a PowerPoint presentation. The central theme is placed in the center of a piece of paper, and affiliated ideas are listed in rapid succession in a

circle around the main theme or idea. With this approach, you can better order your ideas and help your brain work faster to create and list them.

2. **Using the improv/"yes, and" technique**

In an idea-generating session, someone will often say, "Yes, but" and shut down the idea-generating process. All this person has to do instead is say, "Yes, and" in an improv model approach. This one move will keep the idea-generating process alive and stop it from slowing down. This improv approach allows participants to add their ideas to the list and see what happens. The approach comes from improv acting classes around the world, and it has proved effective in a business setting. The process has been known to put participants in a "flow state," helping them break through any barrier or blockage they may be feeling. I encourage you and your team to try the "yes, and" improv technique and see for yourself how better ideas are created on the spot for your high-stakes presentation.

3. **Drawing on diversity of talent**

During a high-stakes presentation, you want to be surrounded by a diversity of talent, people from different cultures and different countries, if possible. Such diversity of talent will produce ideas that are multifaceted and not homogenized to just one culture or talent set. Talent diversity is like a magnet that draws better approaches and unconventional ideas that often become the winning ideas for your high-stakes presentations. Diversity of talent can also help facilitate communication among the high-stakes team members and allow them to expand the boundaries by suggesting ideas that may not have surfaced with a traditional team whose members come from the same culture. You can increase the team's talent diversity by, for example, adding an artist, an anthropologist, or maybe even an artificial intelligence expert.

© Gustavo Frazao/Shutterstock.com

4. Asking the right questions

Asking the right questions at the right time, in the right place, and in the right context can help the high-stakes presenter explore options and solutions for his or her presentation. One typically finds in asking the right questions that there is often more than one answer. Searching for one answer is too limiting and may lead one in the wrong direction, ultimately derailing the high-stakes presentation.

The right questions help you find more creative solutions and provide you with more flexibility to produce different kinds of ideas.

Frank Sesno, a former White House correspondent for CNN, wrote a good book titled *Ask More: The Power of Questions to Open Doors, Uncover Solutions, and Spark Change.* One of the key insights he derived from his years as a top reporter is that asking different types of questions (diagnostic, strategic, creative and scientific questions, to name a few) helped him to not only draw out the best ideas from the top leaders he interviewed, but also shaped the interviews so his audience would benefit from the information.[2] When your team asks the right questions, as Sesno did, you will immediately improve your high-stakes presentation.

5. Using metaphoric thinking to find and link ideas

As you probably learned in school, a metaphor is a figure of speech in which one object is likened to another by speaking of it as if it were the other; for example, "He was a lion in battle" and "She was the heart and soul of the organization."

Work is often associated with rational, linear thinking, the kind society seems to recognize, and play is considered metaphorical thinking, nonlinear, which society views as less serious than linear or scientific thinking. Yet it is play that tends to produce more creative solutions and can lead to the best approaches for your high-stakes presentation.

Metaphors often give us a visual picture that helps us think more clearly about a problem. Let your team try out some metaphors or pictograms, and the results can prove outstanding. One example of the power of a visual presentation with metaphors is the infographic, a tool that shows complex information and data in a form that most audiences can understand. Infographics are becoming the tool of choice for many scientists and engineers who must present complex information to lay audiences.

In their well-referenced book *Metaphors We Live By* (1980), George Lakoff and Mark Johnson illustrated how metaphors shape the way we explain and analyze our cultural life in America.[3] In a high-stakes presentation, the Internet, for example, could be explained as a highway where words and ideas travel across cyber lanes. This type of explanation, a metaphoric mapping, is one of the best ways of explaining the Internet to the average lay person or nontech executive. This metaphoric explanation was used by Al Gore when he talked about the Clinton administration's national information structure in 1993.

6. Preparing a brief/naming exercise

Bryan Mattimore, an innovation consultant and an authority on applied business practices, suggested in his book *99% Inspiration, Tips, Talks, and Techniques for Liberating Your Creativity* that a good way to ensure that your brainstorming session gets off to a good start is by preparing a briefing document. This document has two major sections: the introduction and the creative exercise. The introduction should include a brief description of both the background and goal of the assignment. Also included is a general discussion of how the creative process works as well as reasons for filling out the document. Mattimore prepared six exercises to help find a name for a fictional soft drink:

Exercise 1:

Find an object that represents or symbolizes to you what the naming session is all about. You can draw the object and bring it to the session. Why do you think it represents or is a symbol for this naming assignment?

Exercise 2:

What did you dream of being as a kid? An astronaut? A firefighter? A nurse? A cowboy? List one or more of your childhood dreams.

Exercise 3:

Because of your enthusiasm, the group has appointed you the head cheer-leader for this naming project. You have been successful in leading and inspiring us to create the winning name. The group has asked you to lead a cheer and spell out the winning name by forming the letters with your body. For some reason, though, you cannot remember what the winning name is. You go ahead anyway and form some of the letters that might have been the name. Note: Do not think about the exercise. Just start forming the letters and see what you get. They do not have to be in any particular order.

Exercise 4:

List five names of products or services that you think are great. What specifically do you like about each?

Exercise 5:

Write a nonsense poem about the naming exercise, and yes, it has to rhyme.

Exercise 6:

You are invited to a word party. Think about word roots and pick five new words.

If all this sounds like child's play and is hard to fathom, think again. Mattimore's group came up with PepsiMax in 1993 and developed the brand in Australia, the United Kingdom, and Italy, and it is still on the market today around the world.[4]

7. Storytelling and creative development

Mike Vance, former dean of Disney University, and coauthor Diane Deacon wrote a book titled *Think Out of the Box*, offering seven steps to break the mold and create novel solutions for clients. It is a great tool for high-stakes presentations. The steps are as follows:

1. Create a master plan and overview of the total project objectives, requirements, and deliverables.

2. Develop ideas, with the ideas from the master plan displayed on a titled idea development board. This process is the essence of displayed thinking, an enhanced version of storyboarding.

3. Set up a communication board, a checklist to ensure that effective communications are being carried out.

4. Organize to make sure the details of what, who, and when are not being neglected.

5. Set up a retrieval system, a way to capture past and unusual ideas and other work on projects that might make it into the final mix.

6. Post a briefing board, a visible manifestation that allows an individual or team to communicate and organize daily activities into five areas: do, doing, done, input, and hang-ups.

7. Develop synergy, intentionally bringing together seemingly unrelated ideas into meaningful relationships.[5]

© fizkes/Shutterstock.com

8. **Understanding the culture of the organization**

Culture is the way organization leaders learn about new relationships and build a community. Building a framework for cultural intelligence enhances the organization's ability to solve problems and create novel solutions, allowing it to ultimately succeed when it develops relationships locally and globally and learns how to connect at all levels.

9. **Role-playing for creative thinking**

Edward de Bono, a leading creative thinker and consultant developer, created the famous role-playing model called "Six Thinking Hats" to build discussion around a topic. De Bono believed that diverse points of view create better solutions. He had meeting participants try on different hats to make their points. A white hat was for analytic, objective thinking. A red hat reflected emotional thinking, subjective feelings, and perceptions. A black hat was for critical thinking, risk assessment, and identifying problems. A yellow hat was all about optimistic thinking for the situation at hand. A green hat was for creative thinking and new ideas. A blue hat was for big-picture thinking.[6] A person on the team working on a high-stakes presentation can use De Bono's six thinking hats to find the most novel and innovative solutions for the client. It could help him or her anticipate objections from the client that could derail the presentation.

10. **Practicing skillful listening**

It seems odd, but in school, we are taught reading, writing, and arithmetic, but little if any time is spent learning how to listen to others. Yet much of our success in the professional world is based on our ability to listen and learn what is really going on. The high-stakes presenter can gain the most by putting this skill into play so that the most innovative and novel solution to help the client can surface from skillful and analytical listening at all stages of preparing the high-stakes presentation.

Summary

1. The novelty of the solution is important because it needs to stand out from the me-too solutions often offered in standard presentations.

2. The high-stakes presenter needs to give the organization's leaders multiple options instead of just one solution. This approach gives them the most flexibility to meet their needs.

3. The novel approach, innovation, or idea must have some drama and raise a sense of enthusiasm.

4. The high-stakes presenter must discuss with the client what is working and what is not working. Is it a communications problem, a technical issue, a revenue issue, or tough competitive challenges?

5. The ten approaches to bolster ideation are: (1) brainstorming/mind mapping; (2) using the improv/"yes, and" technique; (3) drawing on diversity of talent; (4) asking the right questions; (5) using metaphoric thinking; (6) preparing a brief/naming exercise; (7) storytelling and creative development; (8) understanding the organizational culture; (9) role-playing for creative thinking; and (10) practicing skillful listening.

Exercises

1. What are the best ways to reveal novel approaches, innovative ideas, and solutions in a high-stakes presentation?

2. In a short presentation (under fifteen minutes) for an entrepreneurial organization, show how you would lay the groundwork with a powerful opening, a well-sequenced theme/argument, and a rationale to meet client needs.

3. Pick five out of ten creative tools in the text and show how they can help the high-stakes presenter build a formidable presentation.

Notes

1. Josh Gordon, *Presentations that Change Minds: Strategies to Persuade, Convince and Get Results* (New York: McGraw Hill, 2006), 171–74.

2. Frank Sesno, *Ask More: The Power of Questions to Open Doors, Uncover Solutions, and Spark Change* (New York: AMACOM, 2017).

3. George Lakoff and Mark Johnson, *Metaphors We Live By* (University of Chicago Press, 1980).

4. Bryan Mattimore, *99% Inspiration: Tips, Tales, and Techniques for Liberating Your Business Creativity* (AMACOM, 1994).

5. Mike Vance and Diane Deacon, *Think Out of the Box* (Career Press, 1997).

6. Edward de Bono, *Six Thinking Hats* (New York: Little Brown, 1985).

PART 2

Mastering High-Stakes Presentations

Communicating Visually, Orally, and Kinesthetically 7

"Tell me and I forget; teach me and I remember; involve me and I learn."

—BENJAMIN FRANKLIN

Effective high-stakes presenters take into consideration the learning style—visual, auditory, or kinesthetic—of their audience members. Neil D. Fleming popularized these learning styles in his VAK model of learning. Trainers and educators have always understood that classroom participants perk up when visual material is connected to the presentation. They have also learned that some students prefer listening to the presentation as their primary mode of learning. Kinesthetic learners, on the other hand, get excited when they can try out a computer lesson or draw an object by hand or computer. Most audiences have a blend of visual, auditory, and kinesthetic learners.

Vision is our dominant way of perceiving the world. After all, our ancestors started the visual age with cave drawings. Archeologists often report that, while the drawings were primitive, they made sense to the cave dweller. The visual stimulation of the brain was what started this interest in drawing. Even today, a good drawing can make a complex idea come alive.

You, as a high-stakes presenter, must find ways to make your messages stand out visually, auditorily, and kinesthetically, the trifecta of your communication arsenal of tools. Today, many of you rely too heavily on PowerPoint, a visual format, to carry your presentations. Instead, you should insert some audio playback or let people try out the product or service. Again, try not to use just a Microsoft template to make your key points (I will tell you more about style in later chapters). Your corporate or organizational identity logos and visuals can help promote the presence of your organization.

When you present visually, you should have eye contact, posture, gestures, and presentation style in mind. You, not your PowerPoints, are the messenger. The message pyramid that David Bartlett includes in his book *Making Your Point: Communicating Effectively with Audiences of One to One Million* is very potent.

Bartlett suggests that it is best to start with the point you want to make, delivered as a memorable statement or sound bite, followed by the message itself, which is then followed by carefully selected evidence and examples. Think: point, message, support.[1]

The message pyramid will make your high-stakes presentation more effective in the age of speed, in which audiences do not have the time nor the patience to figure out what you are saying.

Think about John Kennedy's message given on the occasion of the Apollo moon project: "We will put a man on the moon before the end of the decade and bring him safely back to Earth." Point: going to the moon. Message: Put a man there and safely bring him home.

Your visuals cannot look cluttered or read like a dictionary. You are giving a presentation, after all, not a written document. Remember, less is more. This minimalist approach will make your visual presentation look more professional and be easier to understand.

What makes the visual channel so effective in making your high-stakes presentation work is its ability to engage and grab the attention of your audience. More people remember more of what they see than what they read or hear. The movie trailer is what brings people to the movies, and it consists of mostly pictures and video images. People have a more visual and emotional response to pictures than to a set of written or spoken words.

High-stakes presenters also recognize that showing a picture, a map, or a prop will help gain the support of their audiences. It is no secret that visual communication graphic designers focus on graphically oriented websites to keep audiences coming back. Websites that are word focused tend not to do as well as their visual cousins.

Visual Channels

Think about what you need to do to make your visual channel stand out. Try props, models, graphs, and large photographs to carry the key messages of your high-stakes presentation.

Other visual aids that can bolster your presentation are whiteboards, poster boards, and YouTube excerpts, all of which can engage your audience along the journey.

If you have an upcoming high-stakes presentation, your best interests would be served by watching an episode or two of the Travel Channel's show *Ripley's Believe It or Not*, the program famous for making an audience take a second or even third look at ordinary events turned extraordinary. In one episode, a family firm created a vest for men and women that can withstand the shot of a bullet at short range. This visual dynamic is so realistic that it is hard to believe (yes, it is true). Audiences love drama and challenge.

One of the best ways to make an audience remember your presentation is to opt for something other than PowerPoint and choose to connect with your audience through visual innovation. Authors Cyndi Maxey and Kevin O'Connor, in their book *Present Like a Pro*, highlight the following presenta-

© Haywiremedia/Shutterstock.com

tion. A professor decided to use no markers for his flip chart presentation, instead, employing the invisible word technique. The lecture revolved around six words, which he asked the class to visualize: up/down, near/ far, and here/there. To the professor's surprise, the class knew precisely what he meant.

Another technique mentioned in Maxey and O'Connor's book is to teach invisibly. Attendees were asked to complete this sentence, "A great manager is like [object in this room]"; then each person explained why he or she had picked that object. The participants, according to the authors, remembered 100 percent of the objects and reasons. Our minds store the objects and responses on their own, without the help of formal visuals or PowerPoints.[2]

You can use the room itself, such as its frames, pictures, or window views, to demonstrate business concepts. This hands-on approach is all about connecting with your audience using your visuals for maximum impact.

In his book, *Presenting to Win*, author Jerry Weissman argues that presentation design matters, such as the following:

- Pictorial photographs, sketches, maps, screenshots, and clip art.
- Tables, matrices, and organizational charts.
- Text bullets with short sentences.
- Numeric evaluation, such as numbers expressed as bar charts, histograms, and other more specialized types of graphics.

Working with a graphic designer is often best to make your high-stakes presentation stand out. Good graphics matter in the age of speed to help audiences understand complex ideas and concepts.[3] They also help you share ideas that are popular with general audiences and can be expressed more clearly in graphic form.

New graphic presentation formats from Apple and Microsoft now make it almost seamless to incorporate graphics in a presentation.

We have all heard the saying "A picture is worth a thousand words." Multimedia visual platforms, such as YouTube and Instagram, have accustomed audiences to visual messages that accompany text.

I have found that PowerPoints can add strong visual support to high-stakes presentations, with the following caveat: The PowerPoints you select for your presentation are not the presentation itself, although you may think they are. You are the presentation, and the PowerPoints are just your supporting material, just as the props in a play are not the play itself; rather, the actors shape the play and carry its primary messages. Your high-stakes presentation should be staged like a play, with strong persuasive dialogue, some entertainment, and a powerful closing curtain.

The most powerful presenters in our history, who included John F. Kennedy, Martin Luther King Jr., and Steve Jobs, relied on visual representations to shape their high-stakes presentations.

What role does data play in your high-stakes presentation? You need to share research or data to add credibility to your persuasive messages. Most experts in both technical and research fields make the case that facts and figures are essential for an evidence-based narrative presentation.

But, compared to strong narratives, data pale in significance and effectiveness in high-stakes presentations. As humans, our brains are wired for stories, and we love to listen to them. The ultimate test for whether to use stories in your presentation is to make sure the audience is connected to the narrative and that the stories can help move the audience to action.

Also, one of the best ways to use stories is to frame them as metaphors that the audience can relate to. Remember, you are taking the audience on a journey from A to B to C. High-stakes presenters like using the Swiss knife as a metaphor because it allows them to present the knife's tools, such as a screwdriver, a can opener, a spear-point blade, and a corkscrew in a relatable way.

Karen Dietz and Loris Silverman, in their well-known work *Business Storytelling for Dummies*, suggest that, if you want to use data visualization to move people to action, then meld story and data together. Some of their guidelines include the following:

- Show, don't tell. Leverage the power of images.
- Decide what you really want to happen when presenting your visuals.
- Never assume that your graphics in and of themselves are going to tell the complete story.
- If your data tell a great story, the pictures and graphics don't need to be slick.[4]

Infographics are becoming the tool of choice in data presentations. Work closely with your graphics team to see what works best for your high-stakes presentation.

As surprising as it may seem, one of the best ways to draw attention to your high-stakes presentation is to use a simple flip chart, the tool of choice in the twentieth century. It pulls your audience members away from the PowerPoints and directs their attention to key points that you want to drive home. You can use colored markers and simple graphics and drawings to add variety and emphasis to your pitch.

Auditory Channels

© Den Rozhnovsky/Shutterstock.com

While the visual channel has the most impact on an audience (55 percent), the tone of voice has the next biggest impact at 38 percent, and text and context is at only 7 percent. This research was conducted by Professor Albert Mehrabian to find out which factors most influence an audience during a presentation.[5]

Many participants in a high-stakes presentation learn best through listening, better known as auditory learning. Your tone of voice often influences them and helps them retain important information in your presentation. The pace of the presentation is important to them as well, and, rather than becoming distracted by background noise, it can help the story and data work better together. Many presenters recall their auditory learning experiences from their college lectures and business-related workshops. You can reinforce auditory learning with group activities and use of the Socratic method of pin-pointed questions aimed at arriving at solutions.

You should come prepared to talk through the client's or organization's problems. Show and tell is important, but it is the tell part that carries more significance for auditory learners. Talk to them about what to do and why it is best done that way.

What's more, telling stories gives them additional insights about new ideas and concepts that you want to reinforce in your high-stakes presentation. Telling stories about the heroes in the organization (founder and others) can spark new ideas for the future.

Kinesthetic Channels

As a high-stakes presenter, you are the most effective in your presentations when you understand the styles and strengths of kinesthetic learners. These individuals process information best when they are physically engaged during the presentation through group work, experiments, and brainstorming. Even taking notes, participating actively in discussion, and sharing ideas with others help the kinesthetic learner process information.

You should plan the opening to create interest and expectation, use a series of interactive activities, and provide frequent review and reinforcement activities to dramatize the key themes of the presentation.

Keeping pace with the visual, auditory, and kinesthetic participants in your high-stakes presentation will help ensure that your most important information will be acted on because you will have incorporated the appropriate instructional strategies for various learning styles.

Psychologist David Kolb describes four learning styles that can help you understand the motivations of your audience:

1. The Convergers. People with this learning style have dominant abilities in the areas of abstract conceptualization and active experimentation. In short, they are skilled in the practical application of ideas.

2. The Divergers. Their dominant abilities are in the areas of concrete experience and reflective observation. In short, they are good at seeing the big picture.

3. The Assimilators. Their dominant abilities are in the areas of abstract conceptualization and reflective observation. In short, they are good at creating theoretical models.

4. The Accommodators. They are strongest in concrete experience and active experimentation. In short, they are doers and enjoy carrying out plans in the real world.[6]

Some educators have challenged the VAK model and Kolb's learning styles, asking for more empirical evidence that they work. But, in the practical world of business and consulting, both models share support in helping professional speakers, educators, and trainers understand the learning process and motivations of their audiences.[7]

The primary purpose for communicating visually, orally, and kinesthetically in a high-stakes presentation is to share your ideas with others and move them along to your ultimate goal.

Remember that the participants' experiences as business leaders, scientists, and creatives need to be reincorporated in some way into your presentation. By honoring these professional experiences and sharing related experiences with the audience members, you will gain their trust and more likely achieve buy-in for your ideas and solutions.

Summary

1. Neil D. Fleming popularized the three learning styles—visual, auditory, and kinesthetic—in his VAK model of learning.
2. High-stakes presenters can use the visual, auditory, and kinesthetic channels of learning to help audience members process information that can be acted on.
3. Presentation design matters and includes pictorial photographs, tables, matrices, organizational charts, text bullets, and bar charts.
4. The high-stakes presentation should be staged like a play, with strong persuasive dialogue, some entertainment, and a powerful closing curtain.
5. Data and data visualization can help move an audience provided that the story and data are melded together.

Exercises

1. What are the primary advantages of knowing how the audience members' learning styles help them process the information and data in your high-stakes presentation?
2. Explain how the presentation design tools in the chapter can make your high-stakes presentation stand out.
3. List and explain the four learning styles of David Kolb, which can help you understand the motivations of your audience.

Notes

1. David Bartlett, *Making Your Point: Communicating Effectively with Audiences of One to One Million* (New York: St. Martin's Press, 2008).
2. Cyndi Maxey and Kevin E. O'Connor, *Present Like a Pro* (New York: St. Martin's Griffin, 2006).
3. Jerry Weissman, *Presenting to Win: The Art of Telling Your Story* (New York: Prentice Hall, 2003), 109–21.
4. Karen Dietz and Loris Silverman, *Business Storytelling for Dummies* (Hoboken, NJ: John Wiley & Sons, 2014), 155–57.

5. Bob Etherington, *Presentation Skills for Quivering Wrecks* (Singapore: Marshall Cavendish International, 2018), 14–16.

6. D. A. Kolb, *Learning Styles and Disciplinary Differences* (San Francisco: Jossey-Bass, 1981).

7. Kendra Cherry, "Kolb's Theory of Learning Styles," Very Well Mind, modified November 24, 2019, https://www.verywellmind.com/kolbs-learning-styles-2795155.

Lessons and Takeaways from Toastmasters International and TED Talks

8

"The mind does not work like a camera. The mind works as a projector."

—MICHAEL NEIL, "WHY AREN'T WE AWESOMER?"

As a young United States Air Force (USAF) officer at Hanscom Field in Bedford, Massachusetts, then the Electronic Systems Division (ESD), I was invited to join the Researchers' Toastmasters International (TI) Club at the base and become a part of a group of civilians and Air Force officers assigned to work on major Air Force contracts in system program offices. It was a great experience for a junior officer, and it taught me how to make presentations in both general and high-stakes situations. Multimillion-dollar contracts were at stake, and both Air Force officers and high-ranking USAF civilians had to be at the top of their game. Toastmasters became the training facility on the base at the officers' club to help USAF professionals improve their presentational skills and boost their confidence for high-stakes presentations. I became president of the club, was promoted to the rank of captain, and made some great lifelong friends along the way.

Fast-forward to 2002 in the doctoral program at Columbia University, Teachers College, Department of Organizational Leadership, when I presented my dissertation topic "Transformative Learning in Toastmasters International," I was able to conduct in-depth interviews of Toastmasters selected by northeast regional leaders of the organization who had witnessed deep change in members' perspectives and performance based on their TI training. I will draw on some of those insights and findings in Chapter 15 of this book.

What I learned from my Columbia research is that no matter where you start in your professional/business speaking life, with the right degree of challenge and support in a speaking program, such as Toastmasters, you can rise to the highest levels of your fields.

TED Talk Perspectives

TED talks are given at Technology, Entertainment, Design (TED) Conferences or at one of the many satellite events around the world. Speakers are limited to just eighteen minutes on any topic. TEDx Talks can be organized in local communities, and they basically follow the TED format for speakers. TED organizers look for knowledgeable and talented speakers who have good ideas with a new twist and who can support those ideas with concrete evidence, good visuals, and an engaging manner.

TED presenters often put themselves in high-stakes presentation situations, hoping a broad, international audience will like and support their ideas. Chris Anderson, head of TED and author of *TED Talks: The Official TED Guide to Public Speaking* argues that public speaking matters and will matter more in the future. He points out that speakers from all fields contribute to the interconnectedness of knowledge as is happening now at TED conferences around the globe. Anderson wants to make the knowledge from TED talk accessible to others. In addition, they are important because they are able to show why something matters in less than twenty minutes and to help people fully understand important topics that can influence societal change.

Anderson notes in his book that with the ever-increasing specialized knowledge in our society, we are going to need three things:

1. Contextual knowledge. This is the means to know the big picture and the way all the pieces of knowledge fit together.
2. Creative knowledge. This includes skill sets obtained by exposure to a wide variety of other creative humans.
3. A deeper understanding of humanity. This is a form of knowledge from parents and friends as well as psychologists, neuroscientists, historians, evolutionary biologists, anthropological, and spiritual teachers.[1]

© Siyanight/Shutterstock.com

This three-part formula from Anderson is exactly what is needed for a powerful high-stakes presentation. The high-stakes presenter must perform in classrooms, the boardroom, and government forums.

When presenting, a speaker must have significant contextual knowledge of the topic at hand, the creative knowledge from varied sources to solve the client's problem, and perhaps most importantly, a deep understanding of how humans make decisions and interact with each other. Having only contextual knowledge isn't enough in the age of speed. People can access information with computers or search engines, but the understanding of human emotions and decision making is what makes the real difference in a high-stakes presentation.

A huge contribution of Anderson's book is his five talk tools gleaned from the thousands of talks at TED conferences. The first tool is making a connection and getting personal. People are not computers and want to feel a bond with a speaker, if that is at all possible. It is best to make eye contact from the start and maintain that throughout a high-stakes talk. The TED talk by Ron Gutman on the hidden power of smiles explains that it is important to show vulnerability. This is another important way to make a connection with the audience. People relate to speakers who are vulnerable, just like they are. Two more good pieces of advice by Anderson are to be yourself and park your ego at the door. You may have more expertise than the audience, but it is a poor strategy to flaunt it.

Telling a story is another good way to make a connection with the audience. Chapter 5 of this book focuses on educating stakeholders with powerful stories. As Anderson notes, we are born to love stories, which are instant generators of interest, empathy, emotion, and intrigue.[2]

In creating a connection with an audience, it is best to leave one's politics at home. In today's fragmented political environment, the audience may like your ideas on climate change or nuclear power but might easily dismiss them on political grounds alone, fully ignoring your persuasive argument and solution. Besides politics, Anderson suggests that talk of religion can also put people in shutdown mode. Unless politics or religions are the central themes of your high-stakes presentation, don't let them derail an otherwise powerful presentation.

Anderson's second tool is narration. Anthropologist and Professor Polly Wiessner believes that "stories play a crucial role in helping expand people's ability to imagine, and dream, and understand the minds of others."[3] Anderson cites four key things to remember when sharing a story on stage:

1. Base the story on a character your audience can empathize with.
2. Build tension, whether through making your audience curious or presenting about social intrigue or actual danger.
3. Offer the right level of detail. Give too little and the story is not vivid. Give too much and it gets bogged down.
4. End with a satisfying resolution, whether funny, moving, or revealing.[4]

Anderson mentions the power of parable in his book. Just like the gospels, a parable carries a moral or spiritual lesson. Parables are used effectively by motivational speakers. Norman Vincent Peale, the author of *The Power of Positive Thinking*, a national bestseller, used parables with his audiences, many of whom are traditional businesspeople. Many TED talk speakers use this tool to draw out the meaning of their stories and to help their audiences retain the essential elements of a high-stakes presentation.

The third important tool is explanation, that is, the ability to explain tough concepts. Most high-stakes presentations have a series of tough concepts to explain to the audience. A high-stakes presenter has basically one chance to get it right. Many TED speakers use the introduction or early part of a talk to spark curiosity, which Anderson posits is the first step in a successful explanation. This is important because once our minds open up, we want more information.

TED talk presenter Dan Gilbert, a Harvard psychologist, had the daunting task of explaining "synthesized happiness, prefrontal cortex, and experience simulator." Gilbert says that after winning the lottery or becoming paraplegic, people are equally able to happy. Can this be true? Gilbert explains that this is because our experience simulator takes us to a place we don't expect. Impact bias, another Gilbert concept, is the "tendency for the simulator to work badly to make you believe that different outcomes are more different than in fact, they really are."[5]

Gilbert's field studies show that traumatic events such as losing an election or a romantic partner have less intensity and much less duration than people expect. A recent study shows how major life traumas, if they happened over three months ago, have no impact whatsoever on your happiness, with only few exceptions. Why? "The explanation is synthesized happiness—a psychological immune system. A system of cognitive processes, largely non-conscious cognitive processes that help [people] change their views of the world so that they can feel better about the world's in which they find themselves."[6]

Getting caught in the maze of expert knowledge can take your high-stakes presentation off the rails. Experts in a field of study may become enamored with their own knowledge and expertise and believe that audiences understand their jargon, lingo, and basic elements of the field. The reality is that most people don't, and if we proceed on the assumption that they do, we are in for a rude awakening.

Anderson draws on the work of linguist Steven Pinker to understand how people can avoid the curse of knowledge. Pinker says speakers have to be sure that listeners know how each sentence relates logically to the preceding one, whether the relationship is one of similarity, contrast, elaboration, exemplification, generalization, before and after, cause, effect, or violated expectation, and they must know whether the point they are now pondering is a digression, a part of the main argument, an exception to the main argument, and so on. In other words, Pinker wants the full hierarchical structure of an idea to be communicated effectively. A speaker begins with a web of ideas in his or her head, and by the very nature of language, he or she has to connect it into a string of words.[7]

Experts in communication Chip and Dan Heath address the issue of the curse of knowledge in their book *Made to Stick: Why Some Ideas Survive and Others Die*. They make the point that managers love to tell employees and other stakeholders to maximize shareholder value, but many people are unsure what that means. Top managers have an idea of what that means, but most everyone else is clueless. The curse of knowledge strikes again.[8]

What if John F. Kennedy had used jargon such as "we need to focus on management-supported activities and team-centered programs in the space industry"? We may have never gone to the moon. Kennedy escaped the curse of knowledge and delivered one of the best high-stakes presentations ever on going to the moon at Rice University on September 12, 1962.[9]

The fourth core tool is persuasion. It is no secret that persuasion appears to rule the world. Persuasion, according to Anderson, means convincing an audience that the way they currently see the world isn't quite right.[10]

Former editor of *The Muse*, Alyse Kalish cites five TED talks on how to be more persuasive:

1. "Know Your World and then Ask for It" by Casey Brown
2. "What I Learned from 100 Days of Rejection" by Jia Jiang
3. "How Do I Speak Up for Myself" by Adam Galinsky
4. "10 Ways to Have a Better Conversation" by Celeste Headlee
5. "The Hidden Power of Smiling" by Ron Gutman

Anderson notes that Elizabeth Gilbert also explains how the power of story can be part of your persuasion tool kit.[11] Persuasion is helped along with some humor, anecdotes that humanize you, vivid examples, recruiting third-party validation, and of course, powerful visuals. A strong argument for using persuasion is that logic and reason will take you and your audience only so far. Emotion linked to persuasion is the icing on the cake. After all, most of us buy with emotion and justify with facts.

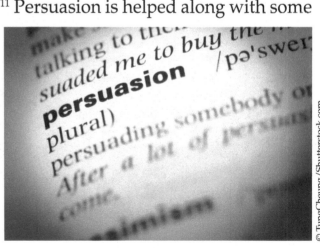

The fifth tool Anderson suggests is revelation. Revelation is also part of the laser blueprint methodology discussed in Part 1 of this book. The audience wants a solution to its problems and concerns and is waiting for you to reveal it. Steve Jobs had a knack for revealing the benefits of new Apple products such as the iPod and iPhone at the right moment to Apple developers and employees and then to the world at large. This strategy was a bit of drama, a bit of show business, and a bit of mystery, all connected with stunning visuals and a major product demo.

In a high-stakes presentation, you may not want to reveal everything at once. You may do it in stages and then magically produce the solution at the end to make it the most powerful element of your talk. This is where creative design and media technology can come together to shape your high-stakes presentation.

Carmine Gallo, the author of the *Presentation Secrets of Steve Jobs*, a *Wall Street Journal* bestseller, has taken on the challenge of capturing the best speech strategies of noted TED presenters. His book, *Talk Like TED: The 9 Public-Speaking Secrets of the World's Top Minds*, explains that the three factors that go into making an inspiring presentation are making sure it is emotional, novel, and memorable.

From the emotional standpoint, Gallo astutely points out that great communicators reach your head and touch your heart. Yet most people who deliver a presentation forget the heart.[12]

In my view, this is unfortunate in a high-stakes presentation. High-stakes audiences typically understand the facts and reasoning behind your arguments. But to convince them to take action, they need to have emotional buy-in. This may come from storytelling, as described in Chapter 5 of this book, as well as from creating a meaningful connection with the audience. Some TED speakers whose talks have strong emotional content such as Bryan Stevenson, who earned the largest standing ovation in TED history and who spent 65 percent of his presentation telling stories.[13]

Another great talk with a significant emotional component is Sir Ken Robinson's talk on killing creativity in schools. It may be the most popular talk of all time with 14 million viewers.[14] The lesson here for high-stakes presenters is to lead with emotion as linked to stories, and you will be on your way to success.

From a novel standpoint, Gallo's research with neuroscientists suggests that novelty is the single most effective way to capture attention. This tool is also part of the laser blueprint methodology in this book. When a high-stakes presenter tells an audience something new and valuable, this information enhances his or her credibility and boosts trustworthiness.

Gallo praised deep-sea scientist Robert Ballard for his seventeen-minute talk about the 72 percent of the planet that is under the ocean. Here are some of the things that the TED audience learned that day for the first time:

1. Fifty percent of the United States lies beneath the sea.

2. Most of our planet is in extreme darkness.

3. The greatest mountain range on Earth lies under the sea.[15]

Why was Ballard's TED talk so successful? It was primarily because the human brain loves novelty, and so will your high-stakes audience. From a memorability standpoint, it is important to remember that if your audience cannot recall your ideas, your high-stakes presentation will fail.

Gallo draws attention to the rule of three in making an eighteen-minute TED talk memorable. What this means is that people can remember three pieces of information well. Giving more information than that leads retention to fall off considerably. Most communication experts recommend the rule of three for talks, making it a good strategy for your high-stakes presentation.

Neil Pasricha's TEDx talk "The Three A's of Awesome" is one of the best examples of how the rule of three works. The three A's he shares with the audience are attitude, awareness, and authenticity.[16]

Gallo points out that the rule of three pervades our lives, as in the U.S. Declaration of Independence, which refers to life, liberty, and the pursuit of happiness, and in the French motto "Liberty, equality, and fraternity." Finally, some of the world's best brands use the rule of three: UPS, IBM, ABC, CNN, and the BBC.

You can make your high-stakes presentation memorable with multisensory experiences. The high-stakes presenter should deliver presentations that connect with one or more of our senses including sight, sound, touch, taste, smell. As mentioned in Chapter 7, communicating orally, visually, and kinesthetically will help make your high-stakes presentation memorable as well.

Summary

1. TED talks are given at Technology, Entertainment, Design (TED) conferences or at one of the many satellite events around the world. TED's organizers look for knowledgeable and innovative ideas on how our society works on all levels.

2. TED's founder Chris Anderson notes that in an increasingly specialized society, we need three things: contextual knowledge, creative knowledge, and a deeper understanding of society.

3. Anderson's five TED talk tools are connection and getting personal, narration, explanation, persuasion, and revelation.

4. High-stakes presenters may not want to reveal everything at once. They may do it in stages and then magically produce their solution at the end of their presentation.

5. TED.com has curated the most popular TED Talks in its history and provides viewers access to those talks.

Exercises

1. Search for five TED talks on how to be more persuasive. Write a short brief on the techniques used by the presenters in those talks.

2. Explain Carmine Gallo's three components of an inspiring presentation. How could you use them in a high-stakes presentation?

3. Search for ways Toastmasters International can help you improve and master your presentation skills in a professional environment.

Notes

1. Chris Anderson, *TED Talks: The Official TED Guide to Public Speaking* (Boston: Mariner Books, Houghton Mifflin Harcourt, 2017), 235–37.
2. Anderson, *TED Talks*, 59.
3. Anderson, *TED Talks*, 64.
4. Anderson, *TED Talks*, 65.
5. Anderson, *TED Talks*, 73–74.
6. Anderson, *TED Talks*, 74–75.
7. Anderson, *TED Talks*, 78–79.

8. Chip Heath and Dan Heath, *Made to Stick: Why Some Ideas Survive and Others Die* (New York: Random House, 2007).

9. http:/er. jsc.nasa.gov.rice talk

10. Anderson, *TED Talks*, 86–96.

11. Anderson, *TED Talks*, 88.

12. Carmine Gallo, *Talk Like TED: The 9 Public-Speaking Secrets of the World's Top Minds* (New York: St. Martin's Griffin, 2014).

13. Gallo, *Talk Like TED*, 41–44

14. Gallo, *Talk Like TED*, 56.

15. Gallo, *Talk Like TED*, 112.

16. Gallo, *Talk Like TED*, 192–94.

There is always a solution. "There are no, 'no's,' just how can I."

—LORI GREINER, *SHARK TANK* STAR

Millions of Americans tune into ABC's *Shark Tank* each week to find out whether potential investors can secure funding from five "sharks," each with extensive business acumen and entrepreneurial experience. It is the ultimate high-stakes presentation situation: a tug of war between the sharks and the investors that hinges on a ten-minute pitch, a proposal that each shark has to consider before he or she makes that multimillion-dollar investment. What makes the challenge so fascinating is watching the varied rhetorical approaches by the presenters in their quest to turn their business ideas into money-making enterprises, in some cases with social benefits to communities and workers. Theories abound on what makes a shark presentation effective.

Alexandra Zissu, a magazine contributor for www.entrepreneur.com, wrote a story that appeared in the October 2016 issue of *Entrepreneur,* "How to Win on *Shark Tank*: What All 495 Pitches Say about Wowing Investors." In her article, she cited Vanessa Van Edwards, founder of Science of People, a human behavior research lab that studied seven seasons of *Shark Tank* presentations, including both winners and losers. Some investors are able to win over the sharks with the force of their personalities and the win-at-all costs attitude they bring to the table. Make no mistake: The sharks are savvy to the

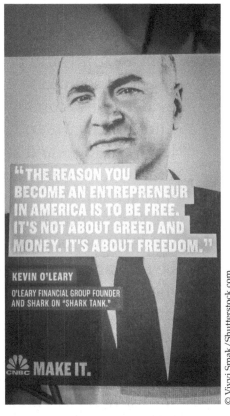

"THE REASON YOU BECOME AN ENTREPRENEUR IN AMERICA IS TO BE FREE. IT'S NOT ABOUT GREED AND MONEY. IT'S ABOUT FREEDOM."

KEVIN O'LEARY
O'LEARY FINANCIAL GROUP FOUNDER AND SHARK ON "SHARK TANK."

CNBC MAKE IT.

© Vivvi Smak/Shutterstock.com

business deals they are considering. Yet, some things matter more to them and make a difference in how they consider and evaluate the presentation.

Van Edwards listed ten big takeaways on how to succeed with the sharks:

1. Know your numbers. Hazy arithmetic on your proposal will more than likely defeat your deal. Sharks turned down more than 60 percent of deals when presenters could not articulate how they would make a profit on the investment. In the business and consulting world, a good grasp of the numbers and data will help you achieve your high-stakes presentation goals. Keep your focus on the business case for your high-stakes presentation.

2. Start with a smile. I know this may sound trivial. Yet 45 percent of those who scored deals had entered the tank with a smile. Add a "hello" and the sharks were more likely to take a deal. In the world of high-stakes presentations, a smile and a friendly attitude can go a long way to achieve your goal. First impressions do matter, and it is true that people do business with people they like.

3. Be interactive. Most notable, 81 percent of successful investors had a product or prop that the sharks could play or work with. Finding a way to engage your audience is almost a must for a high-stakes presentation. This could come in the form of asking questions, showing and talking about a video, working with large visuals and photographs, and of course, demonstrating how your solution would solve a problem.

4. Spin a yarn. Thirty percent of the stories of successful *Shark Tank* pitches included some kind of narrative told by entrepreneur presenters. The evidence is becoming quite clear when it comes to inserting a narrative into a pitch. The audience loves them, and they become inspired to follow your ideas and solutions. We discussed the power of story in earlier chapters. Multimedia storytelling is proving quite successful for news media platforms. The reason this is true is because storytelling and its blend of words, sounds, and pictures resonates with audiences and will do the same for your high-stakes presentation.

5. Be relevant. In 9 percent of "yes" deals, the sharks saw something of themselves in the entrepreneur presentations. These high-stakes presenters found a way to make a connection with the sharks, and you too should make a connection with your audience as a way to ensure your success. Maybe you have something in common with the client, such as the same college degree, growing up in the same neighborhood or city, maybe playing a sport or a musical instrument. One must not

underestimate a connection with the client; it is more likely it will make the difference on whether or not you and your team will get the deal.

6. Entertain at all costs. Sometimes the unexpected, unusual, and maybe even bizarre can turn the tide for your high-stakes presentation. Of course, it must be in good taste to be credible. On *Shark Tank*, the founders of lip balm Kisstixx made Kevin O'Leary (Mr. Wonderful on the show) and Barbara Corcoran kiss. It was a cha-ching moment. Van Edwards notes that the pique technique, a psychological principle, claims humans always prefer the unexpected. Some people may think that working for a corporation requires that they be more conservative in their approach. That may be true, but corporate staff can be open to the unexpected. They are human and will appreciate a novel, unexpected solution.

7. Project confidence. Van Edwards's Science of People team ranked power stances on a 1–5 scale. One is for slouches. What they found is that looking confident gave entrepreneurs an enormously large edge. Those entrepreneurs who were successful had a 3.98 rating for their power stances, and unsuccessful ones came in at 3.83 on average. All the great presentation masters from Dale Carnegie and Norman Vincent Peale to Tony Robbins have told their followers to project confidence as a primary way to achieve success in all endeavors, especially when presenting to an audience.

8. Use vocal power. The Science of People team found that entrepreneurs with relaxed, consistent vocal tones fared better in the tank than those voices that squeal, sound anxious, crack, break, or even drone on. Watch any presidential debate on NBC, ABC, CNN, or FOX, and you will find that candidates with strong vocal power who appear confident usually score higher in the polls as a result of their strong vocal performance. On a scale of 1–5 with 1 being squeaky and 5 being loud and smooth, the most successful entrepreneurs had an average of 4.23 vocal power rating. Unsuccessful ones rated 3.93.

9. Make them laugh. Humor, if done properly, will always carry the day. We want to laugh, even if the presentation has a serious tone and theme. Science of People counted the laughs and found successful pitches had an average of 2.15 humorous moments. Unsuccessful pitches had an average of 1.93. Of the ten biggest deals on *Shark Tank*, four made the sharks laugh during the pitch. Be careful about jokes; it is hard to pull them off and if they fail, more than likely you will lose your audience.

10. Leave the tank. Investors who sought advice before making a final decision on the show had a better chance of landing a deal than those who did not ask for advice. Audiences want to know that the high-stakes presenter has thought through the arguments, messages, solutions, and has third-party validation as needed.[1]

Robert Herjavec, one of the most popular sharks and one who is sensitive to potential investors and the challenges they are facing coming on the show, offered his advice on LinkedIn Pulse in January 2017. He listed five essential tips for selling anything to anyone. Let me elaborate on those tips and apply them to the high-stakes presentation.

Tip 1: The first thing you are selling is yourself. This is especially true for a high-stakes presentation because your audience is counting on you to deliver the goods because so much is at stake. You and your team are the salespeople and, as noted in this book, people often buy from people they like.

Tip 2: Listen more than you talk. In preparing for your high-stakes presentation, the listening phase is important, and if you misinterpret the client's needs because of poor listening, the game is probably over with the client.

Audiences typically have a couple questions they want answered. For one thing, they want to know what they can learn from listening to you. They also want to know what to do with the information and how they can apply it to their situations.

Tip 3: Know who to sell to. In other words, don't oversell to a client who can't afford your solution and who can't make a decision on what you are presenting. Research the participants who plan to attend your high-stakes presentation and find out what their needs are. The investment in time in doing those two things will pay off as you get ready to stand on stage to make your case.

Tip 4: Understand what motivates the other side. Typically, the sharks want a sound investment that will pay off relatively soon after the product or service reaches the market. They also want to know that you and your partners are fully committed and prepared to sacrifice time and money to make it happen. What motivates your client to buy your product or solution? Will it add value to the organization and make it profitable in the long run?

Tip 5: Keep it simple. This includes your presentation style. If you cannot get the central idea across in less than thirty seconds, you probably have lost the audience. After all, this is the age of speed, and people want to make a decision once they are satisfied with the information that you and your team have given them.[2]

Let's consider how six kid inventors made a pitch on *Shark Tank* with their invention, the smart wheel—an invention that would alert the parents of teenagers that their kids are driving with distraction. The model they used was simple but effective in engaging the sharks, and it's outlined here:

https://distinctioncommunication.com/2014/03/25/lessons-from-the-shark-tank/[3]

So what happened? The kids came before the sharks hoping to gain an investment of $100,000 in exchange for 15 percent of the Smart Wheel Company.

After some spirited debate among the sharks, Robert Herjavec and Mark Cuban agreed to give the young entrepreneurs $100,000 for a 30-percent stake in the company with no added conditions.

The fact that six kids with practically no business experience could make it this far is a testament to their skill and confidence. The Smart Wheel has a Facebook page and has been featured on NBC's *Today Show*, MSNBC, and a number of other high-profile shows, all thanks to a ten-minute presentation in the shark tank.[4]

What has the *Shark Tank* show taught professionals about communicating to an audience in the age of speed? Its lessons include the following:

© Rvector/Shutterstock.com

1. Influential decision makers want presenters to help them arrive at decisions as quickly as possible. Practice the rule of three, and stay focused with a good story. This approach will help reduce distractions and keep your audience interested.

2. Presentation style matters. How you look and respond to questions can make or break a deal. The adage "own the room" is essential in the age of speed. The audience is watching your posture and cues for clues that your presentation is on track.

3. Good visuals, props, and demonstrations (show-and-tell) help make the case for your persuasive messages. The audience wants you to paint a picture for them and not wear them down with worry and cluttered PowerPoints. This may be one of the reasons you will not witness a PowerPoint presentation on *Shark Tank*.

4. Having third-party validation from prestigious vendors or corporations interested in your products and/or services makes decision makers more comfortable in choosing you and your team. External publicity in the media, both traditional and social, will boost your chances of a deal.

5. Doing something for society and generating a profit at the same time makes decision makers want to do business with you. Social responsibility matters for corporate leaders and responsible nonprofit organizations.

6. Having a commanding presence, combined with optimism, makes you and your team more credible with decision makers.

7. Humor helps win allies and throws resisters to your ideas and suggestions off balance. A word of warning—the humor must be genuine and not come off as contrived.

8. Adding variety and offering something novel allows you to capture the attention of your audience. It is fine to add a tasteful surprise to your talk; it gives the audience something to remember and talk about.

9. Introducing a new technological advance or algorithm in your talk that will solve the client's problem or challenge gives you a competitive edge in closing the deal.

10. Timing is everything. A good idea whose time has come significantly improves your chances of securing a deal. A traditional and social media presence with influencers who like your products and/or services will help as well.

Summary

1. *Shark Tank*, an award-winning program on ABC, teaches entrepreneurs how to present their ideas in a short time period and gain valuable advice from investors.
2. High-stakes presenters in business, communications, sciences, and other professional fields can follow the *Shark Tank* template for winning audience approval.
3. Storytelling and a strong narrative arc can make or break a presentation. Having the story on multimedia platforms enhances its appeal.
4. A strong power stance, vocal presence, and confidence boost your credibility in a high-stakes presentation.
5. Stay focused and listen carefully to your audience's needs to craft the persuasive messages in your high-stakes presentation.

Exercises

1. Find three *Shark Tank* episodes on the Internet or YouTube, and explain the presentation methods used by the contestants to get funding from the Shark moguls.
2. What does Robert Herjavec, a *Shark Tank* mogul, suggest for selling anything to anyone? How can this apply to a high-stakes presentation?
3. What have the *Shark Tank* contestants taught professionals about communicating to an audience in the age of speed?

Notes

1. Alexandra Zissu, "How to Win on *Shark Tank*: What All 495 Pitches Says about Wowing Investors," *Entrepreneur* Magazine, October 2016.
2. Robert Herjavek, "My 5 Essential Tips for Selling Anything to Anyone," Pulse/LinkedIn, January 24, 2017, Featured in *Best Advice Entrepreneurship, Sales Strategies*.
3. Jim Endicott, "Lessons from the *Shark Tank*," 2014, https://distinctioncommunication.com/2014/03/25/lessons-from-the-shark-tank/.
4. Steve Dawson, "Smart Wheel Update—What Happened after *Shark Tank*," Gazette Review.com, December 5, 2016.

Using Presentation Technology and Media 10

"To sway an audience, you must watch them as you speak"

—C. KENT WRIGHT

More professionals are placing greater emphasis on using presentation technologies to engage and connect with their audiences. This is especially true for a high-stakes presentation. The traditional slide deck presentation is becoming like printed material, and it is only a matter of time before it disappears completely. Its demise will be the result of audiences wanting more interaction with the speaker and a more visual representation of complex information and data. The ubiquitous PowerPoint, of course, will survive but, amidst a wider choice of multimedia options, much in the way that journalism has had to develop multiple platforms to tell stories to diverse audiences.

The high-stakes presenter in the twenty-first century will tap into more video and audio and possibly even animation and expanded storytelling to make their persuasive arguments come alive on the stage and in the board-room. Digitization in the age of speed and rapid communication has altered the way we do things and the way we present to our colleagues and audiences. Marshall McLean's famous dictum, "the medium is the message," may well be the mantra for business executives and professionals required to make high-stakes presentations in contemporary times.

One may also see more high-stakes presentations that are typically reserved for in-person, selective audiences move to online formats and tablets. The bottom line would be to find the optimal way to ensure

the right technology is made available to the right audience, whether it is the private, nonprofit, or government sectors. The PowerPoint versus Prezi debate is often carried out in the classroom by both students and professors and has extended to conference rooms and boardrooms in corporations, nonprofits, and government.

"There are more than 30 million PowerPoint presentations each day."[1] Thus, it is no surprise that most professionals turn to this software to deliver their presentations. It makes the process of creating a presentation relatively easy, for example, with its formatting and design options, which are included in the Microsoft Office suite package. The methodology for designing Power-Point slides can be found at www.microsoft.com and instructional texts.

A high-stakes presenter, however, must be aware of some legitimate concerns about using this program. It has been criticized for elevating form over content and making bullet points the default choice, wherein presentations sound monotonous. The famous catch phrase "death by PowerPoint" refers to all presentations looking and sounding alike.

To communicate messages in both professional and educational settings, technology has ranged from overhead projectors, chalk and talk, and flip charts to PowerPoint slides.[2] Currently, the technology has expanded to computer-aided whiteboards, tablets, Google Slides, and even liquid ink Boogie Boards for presentation settings. In academia and other professional fields, there is also a strong demand for Apple's Keynote presentation software, which presenters can control using an iPhone, iPad, or even an Apple Watch. YouTube and Instagram are the newest tools to help presenters share their ideas with audiences.

The outlier presentation software popular among educators and professionals is Prezi. This software allows for both a linear and fluid presentation of a story line. The presenter, like an artist, creates the presentation on a workspace called a canvas where all the design inputs are visible. Like PowerPoint, Prezi has the capability of integrating text, images, animation, audio, and video. Its key feature is that one can create highly customizable presentations; more details can be found on the Prezi website (www.prezi.com) including tutorials and forums.[3]

Beyond PowerPoint, Keynote, Google Slides, and Prezi, high-stakes presenters can try some of these relatively new multimedia presentation tools:

1. Visme is a cloud-based presentation tool that allows users to create highly visual presentations. It features an intuitive drag-and-drop design method and can feature colors, logos, and images based on the brand of the organization.

2. Haiku Deck is a platform that prioritizes simplicity by creating elegant, basic presentations with high-quality images. It has a library of images and an array of fonts.

3. Pitcherific is a template-based platform for building and practicing a presentation. It guides users through the presentation creation process and prompts them to write out each section of their speeches. In addition, it has a time clock that allows users to track the duration of their presentation to encourage them to fall within a desired range.

4. Canva is an online platform for creating newsletters, media kits, brochures, and infographics and can also be used to construct presentations. Users can choose from more than 1 million of Canva's stock images.

5. Microsoft Events was introduced by Microsoft along with PowerPoint and is used to create live and on-demand events in Microsoft 365.

6. Powtoon is an animated presentation and video platform for creating short informational videos and presentations.

7. VideoScribe is a video presentation platform wherein videos feature a whiteboard and an animated hand that draws different objects and slides in the presentation. Users can easily place objects, insert text, and even draw their own objects or text with VideoScribe's platform.[4]

Another method to elevate a high-stakes presentation is through wearable and throwable technologies. The Myo Gesture Control Armband is a device that allows users to use their movements to transition between slides. In addition, Catchbox is a throwable microphone that makes passing the mic less intimidating through its ability to be thrown across the room to audience members.

What is important to remember is that there is no magic bullet when it comes to making a high-stakes presentation. One needs to test the presentation software that suits one's needs. Costs, design, utility, and overall appearance matter. However, regardless of the software technology, the presenter is still the most important person on stage that the audience esteems to deliver the results.

© Syda Productions/Shutterstock.com

Media Outreach

Sometimes high-stakes presenters want to extend the reach of their ideas beyond a local audience. This means using the power of public relations (PR), social media, blogs, and podcasting. Is the saying "perception is reality—everything else is an illusion" true or false? It depends on one's point of view and the audience's state of mind. Sometimes, no matter how many PR campaigns an organization launches, they can fail because of negative perceptions of the organization and its practices in the marketplace. It is all about the authenticity of one's PR, and the same is true of a high-stakes presentation. PR provides the tools to create influence and maintain positive public perceptions with effective media relations that ensure individuals and their organizations of the third-party credibility necessary for success. Whereas advertising says, "I'm good", PR says, "I hear you are good," and that makes all the difference.[5]

Giving a high-stakes presentation may well mean that media—local, regional, and national—will want to cover it or receive a copy of the talk. The primary criteria for media coverage include the level of public interest your topic generates and the relevancy it has to the media's audience. Important ways to attract traditional media attention for your high-stakes presentation is to be associated with a topic, trend, or fad that has gained currency and may have even gone viral on social media.

Individuals and their teams need to find ways to piggyback onto media coverage by reaching out to editors and producers who will most likely cover their talks in the 24/7 media cycle. New media in the age of speed has rewritten the rules for obtaining coverage; it wants immediacy, relevancy, and interactivity.

Traditional media now offer their stories on digital platforms. For example, broadcast digital news offers immediacy and visual representation. Print news offers depth and detail as well as feedback from its readers. Web journalism presents information on demand and allows for interactivity through the Internet. By including news on multiple platforms, editors and producers can tap into a broad range of readers, listeners, and viewers.

Social media can also extend the shelf life of high-stakes presentations. Not since Guttenberg's printing press in 1439 have platforms such as Facebook, Twitter, Pinterest, Tumblr, YouTube, and Snapchat revolutionized the way information is read, viewed, processed, and delivered to audiences around the world. Their interactive features are what has distinguished social media from the traditional media of the twentieth century.

Social media is no longer seen as a passing fad as pundits and critics once thought. Snippets of a high-stakes presentation on any one of these platforms can allow one's ideas, concepts, or trends to become national news.

It is, of course, a strategic decision on the part of individuals' organizations whether to put their high-stakes presentations on social media. If successful, however, coverage of their talks on these platforms will expand an organization's reach to a global audience.

In addition, many influential speakers have started blogging on their topics of interest. For all practical purposes, blogs have become mainstream and can be found easily on the web, iTunes, and smartphones. Business, consumer, and professional magazines are actively seeking bloggers and giving them access and prime coverage. CEOs of major companies have found that blogging to their customers results in putting a real face on the organization. Many high-stakes presenters who give public addresses now encourage their audiences to use social media. They want the audience to share the ideas of each speech within their respective networks, thereby exponentially extending their reach to a much broader audience.

© mipan/Shutterstock.com

High-stakes presenters may also want to tweet before and after their presentations to make sure their central ideas are covered in real time. Having one's presentation recorded and uploaded to YouTube will boost one's credibility with key audiences.

Finally, high-stakes presenters should consider leveraging their content and ideas into a podcast, a piece of audio content linked to a subscription or syndicated service. If presenters are comfortable with radio, they can readily understand the benefits of a podcast. Listeners can tune in at their convenience and not be held to a fixed schedule.

Technology has drastically changed from the time when public addresses were given by Winston Churchill and John Kennedy in the twentieth century. We now have livestreaming on the Internet through Facebook posts, YouTube videos, and tweeting on national issues. With recent technology changes in the media, the sound bite has dropped to about six seconds from eight in 2011. We no longer have to rely on TV or radio to watch or hear a speech and can instead view it on a tablet or smartphone.

In short, the age of speed has changed the nature of public speaking and, in particular, the high-stakes presentation. One thing, however, that remains constant is that the speaker remains at the center of the presentation and is principally why people show up to listen.

Summary

1. Using presentation technology is an effective way for professionals to engage and connect with their audiences.
2. Digitization in the age of speed has altered the way we do things and present to audiences.
3. PowerPoint, Prezi, Keynote, and other presentation technologies provide tools for formatting and designing a presentation.
4. New types of wearable and throwable technologies improve audience interaction.
5. Media outreach through public relations, social media, blogs, and podcasting will help to reach global audiences.

Exercises

1. Explain the benefits of using multimedia presentation tools for high-stakes presentations.
2. How can wearable and throwable technologies be used in a high-stakes presentation?
3. Suggest ways media outreach can extend presence and brand beyond a local audience.

Notes

1. *How Many Presentations Are Given Each Day*, July 23, 2014, http//www.quora.com/,
2. Barbara Warnick, "Analogues to Argument: New Media and Literary in a Post Human Era," *Argument and Advocacy* 39 (2002): 262–70.
3. Brian E. Perron and Alyson G. Stearns, "A Review of Presentation Technology: Prezi," Sage Publishing, First published online April 8, 2011, Volume 21, no 3, 376–77.
4. Matt D'Angelo, Writing about New Presentation Technology and staff writer for *Business.com* and *Business News Daily*, July 23, 2018.
5. Amanda Barry, *PR Power: Inside secrets from the World of Spin* (London: Virgin Books, 2002).

PART 3

Delivering High-Stakes Presentations

Platform Performance Tips That Work 11

"Everything depends upon execution; having just a vision is no solution."

—STEPHEN SONDHEIM

The right way to launch your high-stakes presentation in the age of speed is to take care of the fundamentals: content design and delivery. Your delivery ultimately makes or breaks your talk. Your platform performance is what connects you to an audience, which helps them figure out how committed you are to your ideas and solutions.

You may recall my reference to the role Toastmasters International played in my early career success and my doctoral work at Columbia University. The Toastmasters experience has also helped executives and professionals around the world achieve public speaking success. Its corporate clubs at Apple, IBM, AT&T, Disneyland, and Silicon Valley have been instrumental in helping executives prepare for their high-stakes presentations. This experience has been replicated at clubs in Rome, Barcelona, and Tokyo, to name a few global cities.

I want to draw on the work of Jeff Slutsky and Michael Aun, who wrote the Toastmaster International guide to successful speaking. In one section of the book, *Talking Your Way to the Top*, the authors suggest four steps for achieving public speaking success.

The first step is creating awareness. Public speaking and your attendant platform performance provide you with a forum to spread your new ideas and solutions in a meaningful way.

Without awareness of what you and your organization can offer, achieving the credibility you need

© Life and Times/Shutterstock.com

for success will be much harder. Your presence at a speaking forum signifies that you—and, by extension, your organization—have the qualifications and expertise to meet your audience's needs. In addition, it is an invitation to make the audience aware of you and your team's capability to solve problems and present solutions.

The second step is fostering understanding. Awareness is important, but you also want the audience to understand your message, and a strong platform performance will help you do just that. Once again, it is all about connecting with your audience to foster understanding and give them permission to believe that your ideas and solutions are the right mix in your high-stakes presentation. A better understanding will help them comprehend and remember the key points of your talk.

The third step is generating impact, a way to reinforce your message and get the audience to buy-in. This is mainly achieved at the emotional level, mostly through the heart and not the head. You must deliver your platform performance in an engaging style that lets the audience feel what you are feeling. Many high-stakes presenters use stories and anecdotes from their personal or business life to achieve the desired impact.

The fourth and final step is motivating your audience to take action. This is essential for a high-stakes presentation and is often mentioned by other communications experts in this book.

In a high-stakes presentation, the audience is waiting for the galvanizing moment when it all comes together for them. They get it, and they want to take action and move ahead with your recommendations.[1]

Sometimes a high-stakes presenter must give the inspirational/motivational keynote address to a regional, national, business, or trade group audience. The stakes can be high, and groups such as Toastmasters International and the National Speakers Association provide special training sessions for

helping speakers enhance their platform performance skills.

The inspirational speech differs from the motivational speech. The inspirational speech makes the audience feel good. The motivational speech, on the other hand, makes the audience not only feel good but also compels the audience to take action.

In the motivational high-stakes presentation, you must establish a style and a presence. Ponder the following questions: Why should the audience listen to you? What experiences can you offer to help change their lives or their businesses? What about differences in the way they live or conduct their professional lives?

I found that the key question many high-stakes presenters ask in training sessions is, "How do I go about developing my motivational messages?" The Toastmasters International guide to public speaking suggests that to be compelling and entertaining in your motivational talk, try using humor and drama to engage the audience. Pick one or the other, and pilot it with the test audiences to gauge their reaction.

Another technique is to dramatize an adversity in your personal or organizational life and how you successfully overcame it. What's more, you can borrow adversity where none exists. If you don't feel you have a compelling story of adversity of your own, you can point to someone else's. You can also quote from a story in the public domain. This approach can give you an opportunity to interview your role model and establish a personal connection.

Here are some additional tips from the Toastmasters International guide:

1. Research your topic thoroughly.
2. Find the right audience.
3. Select a topic based on your goals.
4. Make your material relevant to the audience.
5. Preparation is paramount to power presentations.
6. Organize your content for best results.
7. Develop your unique style.[2]

What do great speakers do that make a difference in high-stakes presentations? For starters, they have exceptional platform presence skills, and they continually improve the ways they connect with audiences.

The Speaker's Edge has published a book on the secrets and strategies for connecting with any audience. Its contributors are leading-edge professional speakers, including four public speaking world champions and one National Speakers Association Caveat Award winner.

Darren LaCroix holds the title of 2001 World Champion of Public Speaking. He writes and speaks about the seven essential habits of mastering presentations:

> Habit 1: Think differently. LaCroix wants us to develop the attitude of a true master speaker. He made a move into the comedy world, and his teachers became life-changing mentors. He also practices what he advo-

cates in thinking differently. He continues to fund and support his own self-development and grow as a professional.

Habit 2: Most speakers give little thought to their introductions. Master speakers, however, understand that setting up the listener is as important as keeping an introduction short. You might start your introduction by offering some personal information to which the audience can relate and that helps make them like you.

LaCroix wants the introduction to answer the following questions: Why should people listen to you? What will they get out of giving you their time?

Habit 3: Focus on connecting with the audience first. Spending time researching your audience and learning about their needs is important. What does the audience expect from you and your organization?

Also try and meet with key contacts in the organization who can help you formulate the strategy for your talk. Without connecting with an audience, you have little chance of persuading them, particularly during a high-stakes presentation.

Habit 4: Provide adequate pauses. Master presenters know that not giving their audiences time to reflect on their ideas and solutions will break the audience connection and weaken the overall presentation. This is particularly true if your questions require them to think deeply about your topic.

Habit 5: Worry bigger. Remember that the presentation is not about you. It is about them—the audience. You must be concerned about the audience's outcome. Will your ideas and solutions close the deal? Will you make them comfortable with you and your team's contribution?

Habit 6: Get lots of laughs. You don't have to be a comedy pro, but most master presenters use a heavy dose of humor. They infuse the humor in their stories if they are not comfortable telling jokes. The humor must be relevant to the talk's main messages and must anchor the key points of the stories. Humor will lighten up the talk and reveal the organization's human side.

Habit 7: Get feedback. LaCroix explains that it does not matter what we say; it only matters what the audience hears. To receive positive feedback from your talk, don't be afraid to experiment with video or powerful photos that illustrate your major ideas. Master presenters keep learning and evolving from their talks and are not afraid to try something new.[3]

© Teera Pittayanurak/Shutterstock.com

A high-stakes presentation can be a proposal at an executive business meeting where senior management from a corporation, nonprofit organization, consulting firm, educational institution, or government are present.

Patricia Fripp is a professional speaker whose clients include corporate leaders, celebrity speakers, and well-known sports and media personalities. *Meetings and Conventions Magazine* named her "one of the most electrifying speakers in North America." She offers a process approach that you can use to create and deliver a high-stakes presentation in a high-level setting.

Fripp has a six-step process for achieving buy-in from senior managers who sit in on high-stakes presentations:

1. Present your conclusion. Senior managers are busy and do not have time to waste. She cited the example of a high-level cross-functional team selected to study whether a company needed diversity training, an important current discussion topic for global companies today that can be expensive if introduced domestically and internationally. For the high-level presentation, she suggested getting right to the point by saying, for example, "Our committee has spent three months studying diversity training programs, and our conclusion is that diversity training would be an exceptionally good investment. For example, we would save money (site dollar amount), increase employee retention by (a percentage) and improve employee morale." In fewer than 40 words, the senior executives at the company knew the bottom line and were now ready for the rest of the presentation with supporting material.

2. Present your recommendations. For example, "The company can initiate a pilot program next quarter as an investment of (x number of dollars). The ABC Training Company has successfully implemented this program at one of our subsidiaries and at other Fortune 1000 companies." Fripp recommends telling the senior managers that all members of the team (cite number of members) have agreed with this

conclusion and that they are willing to be part of an evaluation committed to study the results before a decision is made about a company rollout.

3. Describe what's in it for your audience. For example, show how it will make the company look good by lowering employee turnover and saving money (x number of dollars) at the same time.

4. Explain why this is a good idea in the current business climate (e.g., company cutting unnecessary expenses). For example, remind the senior management of a key company initiative to recruit and retain 20 percent more of the best talent than it did last year. Also remind them that for the last three years, minority associates have traditionally rated their satisfaction 3 percent lower than other populations and that the new program could lower the cost of recruiting and training new associates.

5. Explain how this investment compares to other investments. For instance, the initial cost to roll it out to three offices is only 2 percent of what the company spends for copier maintenance. With this investment, the company should enjoy a greater return than that on other such investments.

6. Conclude strongly and clearly. Fripp suggests saying, for example, that the committee looks forward to answering all the audience's questions and moving ahead with the pilot program.

In sum, this six-step process does everything you need to make your most persuasive case and create a winning proposal.[4]

In his updated book *The New Articulate Executive,* Granville Toogood, a top leadership communications coach and former news producer for NBC and ABC, provides highly relevant platform presentation tips for your high-stakes presentation. They include his five key building blocks for any talk and formulas for designing the perfect presentation. Let's begin with Toogood's five key building blocks:

1. Strong start
2. One theme
3. Good examples
4. Conversational language
5. Strong ending

Toogood always has busy executives in mind who are looking for a big payoff in a short time. He knows that our age of speed is punishing, and he wants the audience to get the message right the first time, knowing that one may not get a second chance in a high-stakes presentation.

Toogood's POWER formula begins with P for a strong punch to get the attention of the audience quickly. Like other communication experts covered in this book, he wants us to begin with the ending in mind, a conclusion with a strong statement to carry your overall message/theme. He believes executives should cut straight to the core of the presentation in a matter of seconds. He wants you to make the bottom line your top line. For example, "America will put an astronaut team on Mars by 2025 and significantly advance our space mission goals."

The POWER punch can include a personal story, a memorable quote, or rhetorical question that galvanizes the audience. The O in the POWER formula stands for one theme. It can be about competitiveness, global outreach, or technology platforms. You can tie your talk's subtopics to your one theme. Toogood suggests using pictures and examples during your talk to prove your case.

The W in the POWER formula stands for windows, a way to see inside the presentation. You must include concept examples, pertinent illustrations, proper data, anecdotes, or analogies to support your talk's overall theme. Because the age of speed is making us a much more visual society, information is increasingly displayed on screens and tablets.

The E in the POWER formula stands for ear. According to Toogood, the best way to reach our audiences is to speak conversationally so that they can understand what we are saying. The high-stakes presentation is no place for the jargon of the business executive, professional, or scientist. It must be straightforward and not pretentious.

The R in the POWER formula stands for retention. Without retention, you will lose the leverage in your high-stakes presentation because the audience will have trouble remembering your key points.

Toogood wants the presenter to have a conversational tone, summarize one to three points, and include a call for action as the best approach for the audience to retain your message.[5]

Summary

1. Platform performance skills connect you to your audience and help you achieve buy-in for your ideas.
2. Groups such as Toastmasters International and the National Speakers Association provide training for professional speakers in all fields of endeavor.
3. Great speakers make outstanding presentations by thinking differently and answering questions such as "Why should people listen to you? What will they get out of giving you their time?"
4. Follow the six-step process in this chapter for presenting information to executive audiences and senior managers.
5. Toogood's POWER formula helps professional speakers achieve their speaking goals in the age of speed.

Exercises

1. Explain the value of the platform performance tips offered by Toastmasters International.
2. What are the seven essential habits offered by a world champion of public speaking in this chapter? Why is this important in the age of speed?
3. Use Toogood's POWER formula to draft a 10–15-minute presentation on a topic of your choice.

Notes

1. Jeff Slutsky and Michael Aun, *The Toastmaster's Guide to Successful Speaking* (La Crosse: Dearborn Financial Publishing Inc., 1997), 1–5.
2. Ibid., 6–13.
3. Darren Lacroix, Chapter 20, "What Does a Master Do Differently," in *Speaker's Edge: Secrets and Strategies for Connecting with any Audience*, ed. Carrie Perrien Smith and Gregory Lay (Rogers: Soar with Eagles Press, 2010), 145–48.
4. Ibid., 121–34.
5. Granville Toogood, *The New Articulate Executive: Look, Act, Sound Like a Leader* (New York: McGraw-Hill, 2010), 37–68.

"When a thing is thoroughly well done, it often has the air of being a miracle"

—ARNOLD BENNETT

The strategic focus of your high-stakes presentation is to understand its purpose, people, point, and place. The purpose is related to why you are doing this presentation. What will you be addressing? The launch of a new product, service, or the company's future?

The purpose: Is the goal to provide information, motivate, or persuade the audience in a high-stakes presentation? It may be all three.

The people: To whom are you delivering this presentation? The target group can make or break the success of your high-stakes presentation. They need to know why they are attending the presentation and what they expect to get out of it.

The point: What do you want to happen as a result of the presentation? What is the evidence that you succeeded and met the audience's expectations?

The place: What venue will you choose to launch your high-stakes presentation?[1]

Most speech coaches are confident in telling their clients that it's all about the arrangements and careful staging that guarantee success. How you deliver your presentation is as important, if not more important, than what you say. A well-executed speech will still fall short if the event staging is poorly planned. A glitch in the presentation software can derail even the most persuasive presenter.

The best approach is for the presenter to take charge of the

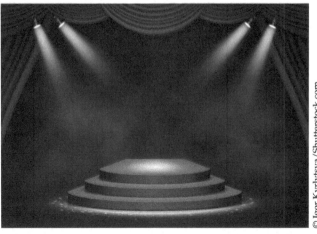

© Igor Kyrlytsya/Shutterstock.com

high-stakes presentation. He or she must assume responsibility for picking the facility and room, checking the equipment and software, meeting with the facility staff, and even, if practical, arranging for transportation to and from the facility. If the presenter relies solely on the resources and advice of the facility staff and management, he or she may be in for a big surprise the day of the presentation.

Marshall McLuhan, a Canadian communications theorist, was right when he said the medium is the message. A well-staged event that runs smoothly gives the audience confidence that the speaker and the organization know what they are doing. It allows for the high-stakes presentation to leave a good impression, close the deal, or make the sale. Most everyone can recall a presentation when the speaker dropped his or her notes, the PowerPoints were in the wrong order, the laser pointer failed, the microphone made strange sounds or no sound at all, or the lights in the room did not work properly.

It is clear—presenters should have control over the operational aspects of the presentation as well as their choreographed stage presence. The staging process must include evaluating the quality of the room so that it complements the level of the audience and the importance of the forum where the high-stakes presentation will take place. The room's walls should be plain without photos, charts, and drawings. It is better if the room is carpeted, a controlled environment, with comfortable seating so as not to impede communications with the audience.

Additional factors should include few barriers between the speaker and the audience. For example, food service providers should be required to do their tasks discretely so as not to disrupt the presentation. Room lighting is also important because the speaker needs to be visible and the lighting must be adjusted during the discussion period.[2]

There are several ways to set up the room for a high-stakes presentation. The following are five models for stage seating that can work for you and your team:

1. The U-shaped model for twelve or fewer people. This model allows for maximum attention by the participants and lets the presenter enter the open space to interact directly with the audience. The presenter can also hand out printed materials and turn back to the screen as needed.

2. The lecture model for twenty or more participants. This model lets the presenter stand on a platform and oversee the participants in the room. The presenter can have two or more large screens with video and audio feeds. This approach has maximum visual appeal while participants can use tablets for feedback if necessary.

3. The theater model, which accommodates fifty or more participants. This model keeps the presenter at the center of the room where he or she can use a variety of presentation technologies and interact with the audience.

4. The horseshoe model. This model is designed for more than 100 people and allows the presenter to establish strong eye contact with the audience and move around the room easily.

5. The auditorium stage model. This model is designed for more than 200 people and is similar to movie theater seating with large screens and an excellent sound system. Personal interaction is limited and the presenter will need staging visuals to support the high-stakes presentation.[3]

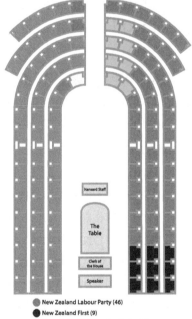

New Zealand Labour Party (46)
New Zealand First (9)
Green Party of Aotearoa New Zealand (8)
New Zealand National Party (55)
ACT New Zealand (1)
Independent (1)

If you are required to give your presentation in an auditorium with 200 or more people, you should make sure the lighting will illuminate you and not cause a dark shadow. In such a large setting, it is also important that the audience knows that you are the pivotal player in the high-stakes presentation.

You should also find out who will introduce you and what biographical material he or she will use. For practical purposes, you may want to send a prewritten introduction

and find a way to stage your entrance. Along with staging the event, the high-stakes presenter must show a strong presence at the podium. You want the audience to be sure that you are the person they can count on.

Leadership is always hard to define and can sometimes be characterized by "I'll know it when I see it." It is the aura the leader presents that inspires confidence that the job or assignment will get done.

In his research with top executives and leaders, Ray Anthony reveals nine core characteristics and traits that project the image of leadership at the executive podium. These characteristics have significant relevance to high-stakes presentation:

1. Decisiveness. Leaders are confident making decisions. They are willing to bear the burden of making the decision and living with it.

2. High stamina and energy. Leaders with stamina keep at their job until it is done right.

3. Honesty and integrity. Faking it or outright lying is a guaranteed way to kill trust and the presentation itself. Moreover, if the audience senses your proposal is self-serving, they will not endorse or adopt it.

4. Confidence and poise. Leaders often come across as confident and poised when they show their ability to control the situation. This also raises a leader's level of credibility and staying power.

5. Knowledgeable and competent. A certain way to impress executives and senior leaders in all sectors of society is to show that you know the topic in all its dimensions. The more you appear to own the topic and are able to control it, the more likely you are to succeed at the high-stakes presentation game. To establish your knowledge and competence, you should not rely solely on the PowerPoints and visuals. Show the audience that you can break away from the setup, steer the conversation, and dialogue with the audience.

6. Understanding and bonding. The best leaders know the unfulfilled goals and needs of the organization and in some cases are able to look deep within the soul of the group to spot its fears, hopes, and aspirations. This deep level of understanding helps build trust and speeds the bonding process—an essential feature of the high-stakes presentation.

7. Big picture thinker. Anthony calls these leaders global thinkers because they have a large-scale view that gives them a complete understanding

of the landscape. Such bold thinking typically involves trailblazers and innovators.

8. Vision creator. John F. Kennedy, Winston Churchill, Martin Luther King Jr., and Steve Jobs believed they had preordained vision that could be achieved to change the world. They took their audiences on a journey to believe in their vision.

9. Passion. Big ideas are rarely achieved by leaders without passion. It is necessary to energize and motivate an audience and sustain their enthusiasm.

Data by itself rarely excites people. Leaders who are passionate show they have the drive to get things done and exhibit a go-for-it attitude. They make the data come alive through stories and real-life experiences.[4]

Few Hollywood movies or Broadway plays would succeed without a rehearsal. The same is true of your high-stakes presentation. In the business world, this is called a dry run, a way for the speaker to receive feedback on the presentation. An evaluation should consider the following aspects of a presentation:

- The big picture. Does it achieve its objectives and contribute to presentation goals?

- Planning. Do the theme and subtopics come through clearly? Are the messages the ones that matter the most? Is it matching the right message to the target audience?

- Organization. Are the introduction, body, and conclusion clear and precise with major points illuminated?

- Support. How are the messages explained, illustrated, and supported? Do the visual aids and stories work?

- Staging. Are the room's equipment, visuals, and essentials handled properly?

- Delivery. Does the speaker come through as believable, forceful, and competent?[5]

© Valmedia/Shutterstock.com

Author and speech coach Carmine Gallo encourages his clients and readers of his books and newsletters to rehearse for an important presentation. In 2019, the Harvard Business School Publishing Company published his advice on rehearsals. I will summarize the key points in the article because they are essential for anyone planning a high-stakes presentation. The five guidelines include the following:

1. Commit to 101 improvements, a philosophy attributed to Google cofounder Larry Page. Page expected his team to create products ten times better than the competitors. The same strategy can be applied to public speaking. If you want to deliver a big presentation, one that is significantly different from your competition, be prepared to rehearse far more than you have done in the past and ten times harder than your peers. The high-stakes presentation needs your most diligent effort. For example, professionals who present at TED conferences do far more rehearsal than the average speaker.

2. Start as strong as your end. Gallo notes that the two most important parts of the presentation are the beginning and the end. The introduction sets the pace for the rest of the presentation and is carefully watched by the audience. The conclusion is what the audience takes away from the talk and how they will judge the presentation.

3. Practice under mild stress. Find a way to move beyond your comfort zone and take the risk to make a great presentation. It is best to simulate the real conditions of the talk as much as possible so you won't be surprised at showtime.

4. Record your rehearsal. You can use your smartphone or ask a friend to record your presentation. This more than anything else will show the areas of your talk that need improvement. You can then practice at home those aspects that can make your presentation better, such as improved eye contact, transitions, and gestures.

5. Ask for feedback. This is often difficult for senior managers in all fields. More and more CEOs are hiring speech coaches or asking their most trusted colleagues to give them honest feedback.

In sum, there is no magic to delivering a great presentation. Rehearsal is the key tool to give you the best chance of making your presentation great.[6]

Summary

1. The strategic focus of your high-stakes presentation is to understand its purpose, people, point, and place.

2. A high-stakes presenter must assume responsibility for all aspects of the presentation including picking the facility, choosing the software presentation technology, and arranging the transportation.

3. Five models for staging the presentation are: (1) the U-shaped model, (2) the lecture model, (3) the theater model, (4) the horseshoe model, and (5) the auditorium model.

4. Leadership at the podium involves being decisive, having high stamina and energy, having honesty and integrity, having confidence and poise, knowing and reaching people, seeing the big picture, creating a vision, and being passionate.

5. Review Carmine Gallo's five guidelines for rehearsal of an important presentation.

Exercises

1. Use the elements of staging in this chapter for a CEO presentation on bolstering reputation in the marketplace. How would you stage this event?

2. Select two of the five seating models in this chapter, and explain their advantages.

3. How would you arrange a rehearsal session for a senior manager in a high-tech organization using Carmine Gallo's five guidelines?

Notes

1. Jennifer and Mike Rotondo, *Presentation Skills for Managers* (McGraw-Hill, 2002), 1–8.

2. Thomas Leech, *How to Prepare, Stage, and Deliver Winning Presentations* (AMACOM, 1993), 168–204.

3. Lilly Walters, *Secrets of Successful Speakers: How You Can Motivate, Captivate, and Persuade* (McGraw-Hill, 1993), 171–92.

4. Ray Anthony, *Talking to the Top: Executive's Guide to Career Making Presentations* (Prentice Hall, 1995).

5. Thomas Leech, *How to Prepare, Stage, and Deliver Winning Presentations* (AMACOM, 1993), 198–204.

6. Carmine Gallo, *How to Rehearse for an Important Presentation*, https/hbr. org/2019/09.

Starting strong is good. Finishing strong is epic.

—ROBIN SHARMA

A competitive high-stakes presentation works well when you have struck an emotional chord with the audience and when you have made a difference in the organization's future. This difference can forge an unbreakable bond between you and the audience.

An adage of success in the professional world is that it's not where you start that's important, but where you finish. After all, the high-stakes presentation is a declaration of intent that the ideas and solutions advocated in the talk will benefit everyone. The organization's leaders are counting on the high-stakes presenter to help them favorably shape the future.

Of course, what the audience remembers is what they will act on. So how the presenter structures the talk and, in particular, the conclusion will influence the outcome of the presentation.

In their book *Made to Stick: Why Some Ideas Survive and Others Die*, Chip and Dan Heath address the ways ideas stick and the way audiences

remember them. They offer the following six principles for successful high-stakes presentations:

Principle 1: Simplicity. This approach means pairing your talk down to its absolute core. When the audience understands your message in its simplest form, they are more likely to get it the first time they hear the talk. You don't have to dumb down the material; you just need to speak naturally and in good taste.

Principle 2: Unexpectedness. This approach works well because it mimics what a movie director does when he or she unexpectedly surprises the audience and takes the plot in a new direction. The viewers will most likely remember the twist in the movie and talk about it later. The same thing is true of the punch line of a joke. It's the surprise that makes people laugh. As a high-stakes presenter, you should think of ways to pleasantly surprise the audience with information they did not expect, but will find meaningful.

Principle 3: Concreteness. It is the conversational language of the talk, not its jargon, that helps the audience remember the core messages and ideas. When presenters offer information that is too abstract, the audience starts to lose interest in the talk. Think of the place where you are presenting your ideas, such as in a lecture hall or auditorium. Audience members have quite a different experience reading a book versus hearing a talk by the author. When reading, they can stop and look things up. In a talk, however, audience members can't go back to the script, so you must make sure your points are clear and concise in a high-stakes presentation.

Principle 4: Credibility. The audience is always judging your credibility based on your knowledge of the topic. Your credentials may carry that day, but more often than not, you will be expected to justify your claims with hard data or influential sources that you can cite in your presentation.

Principle 5: Emotion. This concept is addressed in my Laser Blueprint methodology highlighted in this book. The Heath brothers make it their fifth principle. People often buy with emotion and justify the purchase with facts. Certain images, symbols, and pictures can evoke emotion, and you need to find the appropriate place in your talk to make the emotional approach work for you and get the audience to share your feelings.

Principle 6: Stories. This approach puts a high priority on storytelling to achieve buy-in with the audience. The Heath brothers have it as one of their key principles for making ideas stick.

© buffaloboy/Shutterstock.com

From the storytelling traditions of our families to Hollywood movies, we love sharing stories. Many high-stakes presenters introduce stories into their presentation narratives to help them become memorable and draw the audience closer to them.[1]

Top speech coaches often agree that the most critical point in any presentation is the close. Audiences remember most what is said at the beginning and end of the talk. Therefore, a strong finish should include the following:

1. Restate the big idea or theme of the talk. Remind the audience why they came to hear you and how they can benefit from what you said.

2. Summarize the three main points of the talk. The rule of three states that three is the smallest number required to make a pattern. It is used by copywriters and PR executives to make persuasive arguments, and it helps communicate complicated ideas effectively.

3. Offer a novel solution to the organization's problems and challenges. It supports the approach offered in this book's Laser Blueprint methodology—it makes your talk relevant to the needs of the organization.

4. Provide an appeal to action that helps the audience take the required steps to move ahead. Be succinct with your advice.

5. End on a positive note by sharing a personal story, anecdote, or quotation. Let the audience go home with a good feeling about you and your organization.

The age of speed has changed the way audiences hear and react to presentations. They want the presenter to get straight to the point, they don't want to be overwhelmed with PowerPoint slides, they want the messages to be clear so they can understand them, and they want to leave with a clear understanding of what is expected of them.

They live in a social media world of tweets, texts, and apps where the messages are available to them in real time. High-stakes presenters need to recognize the new social media construct and incorporate it into their presentations accordingly.

In a high-stakes presentation, the presenter must decide whether to take questions as they come up or save them for the end. There is no one right answer to this situation. It depends on your judgment and the dynamics of how the presentation is going. But the one thing you can do is plan for the questions.

Jennifer and Mike Rotondo, in their book *Presentation Skills for Managers*, offer a five-step process for handling questions that are particularly relevant to the high-stakes presentation:

1. Anticipate the questions that might come up. You have done a reconnaissance of the audience—their needs, challenges, and outstanding issues—now put yourself in their position and list the questions their senior managers and teams might ask. You can hold a mock question and answer (Q&A) session with your team to test the waters on what might show up. You can also pose a question that you know they are likely to ask during your presentation.

2. Listen carefully. You want to make sure you get their questions right the first time. If you are not sure you understand the question clearly in your mind, you can ask for it to be repeated. When you get negative or hostile questions, you should maintain control of your emotions and give the best answer without becoming defensive. Sometimes a pause can work wonders by giving you time to think and respond.

3. Repeat or rephrase. The reason for a repeat or rephrase, according to the Rotondos, is to verify your understanding, to maintain control of your emotions, and to buy time to think about your answer.

    You should always try to show the person asking the question that you respect him or her and that you want others in the audience to feel free to raise questions as well.

4. Answer clearly and concisely; I might add honestly as well. If your answer is complex, you should structure it around the "talking points" that you have prepared in advance. Stay away from jargon, and repeat the key points you covered in the presentation.

    You may want to refer to experts who support your position. After all, they will add third-party credibility to your answer.

5. Go to the next question as diplomatically as possible. Once you finish your answer, look around the room to signal you are inviting other questions. You can, of course, answer a follow-up question, but then you should move on quickly so that one person does not dominate the proceedings.

Keep track of the time of the Q&A session. Don't let it go too long and always end on a positive note.[2]

Suzanne Bates, who works with top executives from major companies, has written a book titled *Speak Like a CEO.* In it she cites types of tough questions the high-stakes presenter can encounter in speaking situations. They are as follows:

1. The false alternative. This question presents two or more equally wrong or inaccurate scenarios from which you are asked to choose the false alternative. Respond by being factual in your answer and refute what is implied in the false alternative.

2. Irrelevant questions. These types of questions are not remotely connected to your presentation topic. The questioner wants to take you down a path you don't want to go. You can politely suggest that the question might be handled in another forum, but not at this time. You could also say, "I will follow up with my senior management and get back to you."

3. Hypothetical questions. This type of situation is impossible to predict but unlikely to happen. To answer this type of question, you can point out that you won't entertain a hypothetical situation because it may never happen. Then move on to the next question.

4. The anonymous source. The questioner can suggest a rumor he or she heard about layoffs or downsizing at the organization. You can point out that this is pure speculation, and the organization will always be frank with its employees on sensitive issues and respond accordingly.

Bates offers the 98 percent solution to be better prepared for the Q&A session. She recommends that you think like your worst critic and hard-nosed skeptic and write down the questions you wish no one would ask and that could throw you off your performance.

Even with your best preparation, the other 2 percent can surprise you and make you look less confident. The work around for the 2 percent challenge is to talk to as many people as possible in the organization who can help you sort out the surprise questions.[3]

In *The Master Communicator's Handbook*, Teresa Erickson and Tim Ward share their advice for answering questions effectively. Let's review their approach and how it can be applied to high-stakes situations.

1. Answer the question. First, give the audience a direct answer to the question. You should not equivocate with extraneous or background material.

The authors note that a direct answer up front gives your audience more confidence that you know what you are talking about and that you are not trying to evade them.

Some cultures may prefer an indirect approach to answering a question. Cultural context does play a role, particularly in Asia. Tone and body language can count as much as or more than words spoken.

2. Make your message clear and concise. Once you answer the question, you should link it to the key talking points of your presentation. The reason for this approach is that you want to achieve the strategic objective of the talk and create buy-in from the audience.

3. Back up your answer with one good example. Don't make your answer so complex that only an expert would understand it. Visuals in the Q&A session can help the audience remember your answer and stay connected with you.

4. End well. Try and wrap up your answer under a minute if at all possible. The exchange with the audience should be lively and show that you are finishing strong. It can be helpful to give them a prompt such as "to sum up" and then end quickly.[4]

Mortimer Adler, author, philosopher, and educator, in his book *How to Speak How to Listen*, points out that persuasion is most effective when followed by a Q&A session. He notes that the Athenian Agora and the Roman Forum were places where citizens reacted to a speech, asking question and responding to answers. Most advertised lectures and talks in the United States today are followed by Q&A sessions. The high-stakes presentation at a business forum is also followed by a Q&A session.

Adler claims that he learned the most from his lectures and presentations from the Q&A sessions. More specifically, he learned what points need to be more fully explained, what arguments need more amplification, and what ideas need to be more succinctly stated.

Adler is very astute in pointing out that the learning that takes place in the Q&A session is important intelligence and that the presenter should look forward to it, not try to avoid it. What the audience tells the presenter will lead to improvements in both style and substance.

Even when objections are raised by the audience, presenters can test their own thinking process and find out where they have been mistaken or inadequate.

Finally, the high-stakes presenter should try to answer or draw out any questions that indicate resistance. Doing this may seem counterintuitive, but by drawing out resisters and asking them questions, you reassure your audience that you have the confidence and skill to handle even the toughest questions.[5]

Summary

1. Chip and Dan Heath's "Made to Stick" principles are simplicity, unexpectedness, concreteness, credibility, emotions, and stories.
2. Crafting stories helps high-stakes presenters win over and draw audiences closer to them.
3. A strong finish for your presentation should include the following: (1) restate big ideas, (2) summarize three main points, (3) offer a novel solution, (4) offer an appeal to action, and (5) end on a positive note.
4. The high-stakes presenter needs to recognize the new social media construct and focus on presentation goals.
5. The following is the Rotondos' five-step process for hard questions: anticipate the questions, listen carefully, repeat or rephrase, answer clearly and consistently, and go to the next question.

Exercises

1. Explain how Chip and Dan Heath's "Made to Stick" ideas can be used in a high-stakes presentation.
2. List the presentation tools offered in the chapter to finish strong in your high-stakes presentation.
3. List six ways to handle the Q&A session in your high-stakes presentation.

Notes

1. Chip Heath and Dan Heath, *Made to Stick: Why Some Ideas Survive and Others Don't* (New York: Random House, 2007), 14–19.
2. Jennifer Rotondo and Mike Rotondo, Jr., *Presentation Skills for Managers* (McGraw Hill, 2002), 150–65.
3. Suzanne Bates, *Speak Like a CEO: Secrets for Commanding Attention and Getting Results* (McGraw Hill, 2005), 121–32.
4. Teresa Erickson and Tim Ward, *The Master Communicator's Handbook* (Changemakers Books, 2015), 57–66.
5. Mortimer J. Adler, *How to Speak How to Listen* (Collier Books, MacMillan Publishing Company, 1983), 115–25.

All your strength is in union; all the danger is in discord

—Henry Wadsworth Longfellow

I n the age of speed, more organizations are asking for a team presentation, especially in high-stakes situations. The prime reason is that it gives the organization a chance to see a team in action, a mirror of how they will perform if they are assigned a project.

The casting of a team is important, particularly the team leader, in a high-stakes presentation. A lot of emphasis is often placed on individual competence, as it should be. Yet, when it comes to team competencies, the bar is not as high.

The Margerison-McCann team competence model is an excellent tool to access how a team will perform in a variety of scenarios. The short definitions and questions provided by Charles Margerison, creator of the model's nine competencies, are as follows:

1. Advising. Gathering and reporting information. How well do your team members provide advice to each other and people outside of the team?

2. Innovating. Creating and experimenting. To what extent do your team members do the job as outlined, or do they look for ways to make improvements through innovation?

3. Promoting. Exploring and presenting opportunities. All teams have to promote what they do and influence others. How well does your team do this?

4. Developing. Assessing and testing new approaches.

Ensuring that systems and products are well developed takes time and requires considerable linking skills, internally and externally. How does your team ensure that systems and products are well developed?

5. Organizing. Arranging how things will work. Implementing any plan requires an organization and a systematic approach. How does your team do this?

6. Producing. Making and delivering outputs. Nothing is finally achieved until something is produced. This requires a lot of internal team linking, but also external linking with suppliers. How does your team perform?

7. Inspecting. Controlling and auditing the working systems. This activity is not always the most popular. How effective is your team at conducting the inspection and linking with others to ensure they gain support?

8. Maintaining. Upholding and safeguarding standards and processes. All operations require physical and professional maintenance. How well does your team perform in this area?

9. Linking. Coordinating and interacting with others. How well does your team do this?

In highly complex and integrated systems, including in business, the military, and nonprofit organizations, the Margerison-McCann team competency model will support the novel solutions and ideas offered by the high-stakes presentation team and are backed by members of the team who know how to find the right information and who can respond quickly.[1]

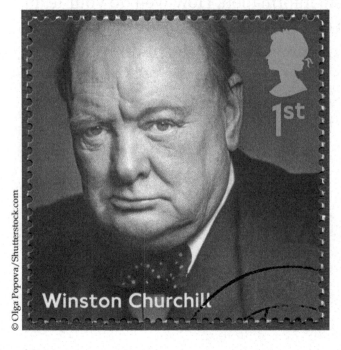
© Olga Popova/Shutterstock.com
Winston Churchill

Teamwork and successful team presentations are often linked to the transformation of its leader. A leader is responsible for the team's motivation in crucial situations, the team's reaction to obstacles, and the team's performance in regard to the assigned mission.

The team leader, whether a great politician such as Winston Churchill or a business leader such as the former chairman and CEO of GE, Jack Welch, understands the need to

Jack Welch, Former Chairman and CEO of GE

establish a vision of the organization's capability, create the culture in which motivation can happen, and ensure the message is implemented on the right platforms.

The team leader knows whether his or her team needs to inform, persuade, celebrate, and share important ideas or present novel solutions. Perhaps the most important trait of team leaders is to establish credibility for themselves as well as the team.

In the age of speed, a leader's credibility may be the primary currency because it helps establish the accountability the organization brings to the assignment and the importance of not overpromising more than the team can deliver.

According to John Baldoni, author of *Communication Secrets of Great Leaders*, four important things are critical to the leader's message:

1. It informs people of what the issues are and what they need to do.
2. It involves others by soliciting their input.
3. It invites people to think about what they can do to make things better for themselves and their organizations.
4. It ignites people to participate in the enterprise, whether through fulfillment of a goal or the transformation of a culture.[2]

The team leader and chief presenter work best when three team processes are in place. The first is team cohesion. This signals that its members are highly involved in team activities and are likely to remain with the team. Team cohesion often leads to higher satisfaction and interaction with other members.

The second process is team communication. Team members listen well, are open to suggestions, and receive feedback well. A team can fail when it lacks good communication and fails to take direction.

The third is the appropriate handling of conflict management. Nothing hurts a team more than unresolved tension because it impedes the team from clear thinking and making sound decisions.

The combination of a good team leader and strong teamwork will determine how well a team performs in the age of speed. Organizations want to hire and work with teams who work well and have a shared vision for their goals.[3]

Jon Steel, advertising executive, author of *Perfect Pitch*, and winner of the London 2012 Olympic site selection team pitch bid, offers his advice on team pitching, which translated into commercial success. His new business model team pitch is called RASCI.

R is for responsible. Every pitch team has a leader who sets the tone and direction of the team. For example, he or she makes decisions on the resources that will be required, the budget, and the timing.

Steel points out that the leader selects the team on the basis of individual expertise and the likelihood of the people working well together.

A is for approve. On every project someone should be clearly identified as the individual who has final approval. This person provides encouragement and backs up the leader with the resources to complete the job.

S is for support. These are the people the leader needs to get the job done. It may include support staff, editors, and producers of collateral material.

C is for consult. The team may provide outside expertise to get the project done, such as a psychologist or technical expert, depending on the client's needs.

I is for inform. The team must keep the appropriate people informed, even if they are not directly involved in the pitch. They should be aware of the key issues and the progress made on the proposal. They may not be asked to make decisions, but their influence and counsel may be needed during the team pitch process.

Steel makes clear that the RASCI process improves clarity, accountability, and teamwork—all necessary ingredients for a successful team presentation.

This RASCI process can be particularly effective in the age of speed because agencies and consultancies are under extreme pressure to deliver results, and the pitch team needs all the help it can get.

The team cannot succeed alone with only technology, such as Skype, voicemail, or social media. The team needs to work very closely together and participate in all team activities.

© Rawpixel.com/Shutterstock.com

Solo performances may work in some scientific fields, but the team will always outperform the individual in creating faster and better ideas.[4]

Twenty-first century organizations are continually looking for ways to build teamwork to improve team performance. Let's review some of the approaches:

1. Social activities that include a nonwork-based event. Popular examples are team lunches and celebrations.
2. Sporting activities. Sports create team cohesion. Touch football, golf, and tennis are popular with teams.
3. Adventure activities. This type of activity takes a team out of their comfort zone and helps them build morale. Popular activities are often obstacle courses and rock climbing.
4. Planning activities as a way to have a shared vision and teamwork plan.
5. Communication activities are valuable for enhancing relationships, creativity, and interpersonal communication skills. This can include team presentations and improvisation activities.
6. Problem-solving activities are designed to build analytical, creativity, and emotional intelligence skills. It could include brainstorming tasks or team projects.
7. Trust, rapport, and emotional intelligence activities. This can include facilitated group reflection and rapport building.

It is important for organizations to recognize that these activities may not work for every organization or every team. The culture of the organization will dictate which activity works best for the organization hosting it.

What makes many of these team-building activities work is the fun component, which strengthens the individual connection and makes the learning experience come alive. One of the latest trends in team building is gamification. It uses game mechanics and simulation to create a fun and educational experience. Video gaming has been popular in the United States and overseas markets, and it gives participants tasks to solve in a competitive landscape.[5]

Team building is a process that leads to a successful team presentation and a collaborative effort on the part of participants involved in a mutual subject of interest. The team, if structured properly, will come up with more ideas than the solo presenter. However, it must have clear goals, realistic boundaries, and a plan of action to succeed.

A good plan takes into account the purpose of the presentation, the requirements, the specific needs of the audience, the key decision makers coming to the event, and the key issues and hidden agendas the team will face.

Thomas Leech, a leading consultant and communications coach, notes that there are several factors for producing effective team presentations. They include the following:

1. Understand how the presentation fits into the overall communications scheme. Can it stand alone, or does it work with written reports that provide most of the detail? This is particularly important for the high-stakes team presentation. The team agrees on the umbrella theme of the talk.

2. Recognition of the importance of the presentation and the energy that will be required to pull it together. The team needs to figure out what is required up front to avoid confusion later on.

3. Getting a head start by considering what it is going to take to win. Like a chess master, the leader and his team must know all of the key moves ahead of time. Who will be the likely speakers, and what is their talent for the task? What presentation technology will work best for this client or organization? In this scenario, trial run presentations must be planned with enough time to make revisions and changes in the talk.

4. Early direction and frequent reviews by leadership: Don't wait too long to shore up a weak presentation or make a good presentation an outstanding one. Keep the process fluid for changes to be made as necessary.

5. Support from upper management of the program manager or team leader: The team and audience must sense that the program manager or team leader has the support of top management and can act on their behalf.

6. Recognition by everyone of the team's focus. All ideas and contributions must be considered by the team because they can have a significant impact on the overall result.

7. Treatment of content that recognizes that the audience is probably a team too. Team presentations often draw audiences more diverse in level and discipline than single-speaker presentations.

8. Getting to know each other: It is important for teams to socialize with each other and share in success together.

9. Careful attention to operational detail: Be prepared for the occasional mishap in a twenty-minute presentation. The team should stay focused on the details to make the high-stakes presentation work.[6]

Some of the same rules covered in this book for single presenters of high-stakes presentations apply to team presentations. The preparation should include the following:

1. Select a strong moderator to lead the team to produce a cohesive presentation.

2. Understand the audience, its needs, and its decision makers.

3. Build a powerful introduction, body, and conclusion, including stories to engage the audience.

4. Create staging and presentation technologies that meet the needs of the audience.

5. Rehearsing the presentation and Q&A several times before the final event.

Summary

1. In the age of speed, more organizations are asking for team presentations to learn how they will perform in a variety of scenarios and how they will help find solutions to their challenges and problems.
2. The Margerison-McCann team-building model includes advising, innovating, promoting, developing, organizing, producing, inspecting, motivating, and linking.
3. Teamwork and successful team presentations are often linked to the transformational skill of the leader.
4. John Steel's business team pitching model is called RASCI. R is for responsible. A is for approval of every aspect of the team project. S is for support and resources to get the job done. C is for consulting with outside expertise. I is for informing the appropriate leaders on the key issues and progress of the pitch.
5. Team building and team presentations are intrinsically linked as a collaborative effort on the part of the participants to deliver a winning presentation.

Exercises

1. Explain the components of the Margerison-McCann model and how it can be helpful in team-building activities for high-stakes presentations.
2. What is the role of transformational leadership in helping a team succeed?
3. Advise a team leader on the best ways to prepare for a high-stakes team presentation using the tools and team-based rules covered in this chapter.

Notes

1. Charles Margerison, "Team Competencies," *Team Performance Management Journal* 7, no. 7/8 (2001): 117–22.
2. John Baldoni, *Great Communications/Secrets of Great Leaders* (McGraw-Hill, 2003), 27–40.
3. Shelly D. Dionne, Francis J. Yammarino, Leanne E. Atwater, and William D. Spangler, "Transformational Leadership and Team Performance," *Journal of Organizational Change Management* 17, no. 2 (2004): ProQuest Central Log, 177.

4. Jon Steel, *Perfect Pitch: The Art of Selling Ideas and Winning New Business* (John Wiley and Sons, Inc., 2007), 155–57.

5. Ann Keavney, *Team Building Strategies, Training and Development*, www.amtd-au, April 2016, 26–28.

6. Thomas Leech, *How to Prepare, Stage, and Deliver Winning Presentations*, 3rd ed. (AMACOM, 2004), Chapter 16.

Shaping the Future: Face-to-Face, Virtual, and Blended Learning Presentations

15

"The best way to predict the future is to create it"

—ABRAHAM LINCOLN

While at Columbia University, I completed my dissertation on transformative learning in Toastmasters International (TI), one of the largest nonprofit organizations in the world devoted to helping people learn or master public speaking and leadership skills. I conducted more than one hundred interviews with TI members, senior leaders in the organization, and presidents of Toastmasters chapters in the United States.

My research study was designed to ascertain how far-reaching changes had occurred with TI members and how those changes had significantly affected their personal and professional lives. My study sample included TI members who were nominated by chapter officers and senior members of the organization based on having experienced significant changes and made great achievements by participating in the TI program.

I wanted to discover if those members had had a transformative learning experience. In its simplest definition, transformative learning is deep change that promotes a perceptible shift in an adult learning perspective. It stimulates new thinking that leads to a willingness to take risks, challenge old assumptions and beliefs, try new roles, and make new meaning.

For high-stakes presenters to be successful in the twenty-first century, they need to cope with radical changes in organizational life and society.

One of the major findings of my study was that TI embedded challenge and support in its learning

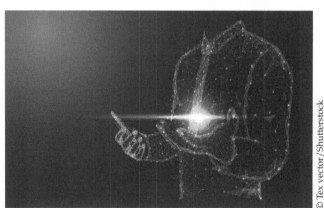

materials that allowed its members to take risks and grow in their work and life endeavors. Most interview participants said that they could not have experienced a deep change in TI had they not been challenged and supported in its learning environment.

Many of the challenges and supports in the program leading to deep change could be linked to the coaching and mentoring conversations that helped members refine distorted perspectives of thought and replace them with new frames of reference. These conversations and TI learning materials were instrumental in helping members fundamentally reshape their worldview so that they could move to a new level of thinking that resulted in new possibilities and deep change.

Members were able to question who they were, what they did, and why they did it. The participants who experienced deep change were able to make dramatic shifts in their personal and professional lives as a result of transformative learning in TI.[1]

High-stakes presenters must be willing to take risks and gain valuable feedback from others to help make their presentations a cut above the rest and a valuable contribution to the organizations they serve.

The future of high-stakes presentations is being shaped by face-to-face, virtual, and blended learning approaches.

Face-to-Face

Face-to-face presentations are still the most direct way to reach an audience, help solve its problems, and offer novel solutions. The late Malcolm Knowles, a leading adult educator, argued that the success of face-to-face presentations in large meetings hinges on the platform itself, the audience, and the relationship between the two. He wanted the face-to-face presenter to upscale the amount of interaction by adding a chalkboard (now a whiteboard), flip chart (now dominant visuals), and film strip (now video enhancement). He understood that the audience's attention would wander unless interaction was maintained. He encouraged adding another person to interact in a debate, dialogue, or interview. He advocated panel discussions, group interviews, dramatic skits, or demonstrations.[2] It is no surprise that Steve Jobs of Apple followed a similar

© melitas/Shutterstock

formula in his presentations to large audiences, and this became a prominent model for important presentations in the business world.

The interaction between the platform and the audience can be enhanced by bringing members of the audience to the platform for reaction to the proposal or as watchdogs to comment on the proposal when it is completed. The high-stakes presenter should want the audience to psychologically identify with the interaction on the platform.

Finally, interaction among members of the audience can be illustrated in several ways. For example, speakers can ask some members of the audience before the presentation to pool the questions or issues they would like them to address and have one member summarize the results. This gives high-stakes presenters a good idea of where the audience wants to go.

Most presentations are unidirectional in that the speaker talks directly to the audience and waits for the Q&A to find out what the attendees are thinking. Face-to-face presentations can be far more effective if speakers have some idea of what the audience is looking for and can direct their remarks to meet those needs.

The primary aim of future presentations should be to move away from unidirectional presentations to facilitating dialogue with the audience (two-way dialogue) including use of advanced technologies to make this happen.

Some trends to watch for in the future include:

1. Learning to communicate data clearly; showing the link between data and story.
2. Projection mapping onto 3-D objects.
3. Using virtual reality (VR) and augmented reality (AR) to create immersive experiences.
4. Narrating the audience's journey with clarity, conviction, and, most of all, empathy.
5. Creating movie-related content; adding a printed version of the slides.[3]

Virtual Presentations

Virtual presentations are starting to play a more significant role in high-stakes presentation scenarios for

organizations. Even highly competitive face-to-face presenters are starting to notice the impact of using electronic presentations in forums that reach high-level participants and stakeholder audiences.

How is it possible to engage and persuade an audience you cannot see? First, the electronic presentation must be in tune with the audience's attention span to offer an effective visual experience. Furthermore, the virtual presenter still must sell, teach, or tell a story to the online audience.[4]

Dr. Joel Gendelman is a thought leader on the innovative use of communications technologies. In his book *Virtual Presentations that Work*, he has created a template for electronic presentations that has relevance for the high-stakes presenter.

Here are some of Gendelman's insights and strategies for the virtual presentation:

1. Deliver virtual presentations that make it about the audience. This can be the role of the producer/moderator, who should handle the technical aspects of your presentation and all the tools involved. This person can function as an announcer introducing you and other participants, moderating the Q&A session during and after the presentation, and enforcing the ground rules of the presentation. You may recall the role of the sidekick on late-night television and how that person helped move the program along. The virtual producer should also test the slides, media assets, URLs, and stored handouts to ensure the audience's experience is not disrupted by a glitch.

2. Gaining attention and establishing relevance in an electronic presentation will be harder to do than in a face-to-face presentation. Gain the audience's attention in the first thirty seconds, and the material needs to be relevant and answer the questions that are on the mind of the audience. One way to get people's attention can be with a strong visual, powerful quote, or compelling statistic. Another good tactic for gaining attention is to demonstrate your casual style and your intention to make a difference. You can also employ movie and audio clips to set the tone for the presentation.

3. Identify objectives and set expectations. In the early part of the virtual presentation, set the ground rules and tone. Start by listing the goals and objectives of the meeting up front and include a schedule. It is acceptable to ask for feedback on how everything is working.

4. Know how to present information in a virtual presentation. A virtual presentation should have a variety of communication elements. One option

is to introduce a multimedia presentation using Adobe Captivate, Flash, or Dream Weaver. Also, you can ask the audience to share their stories using their chat or audio feeds.

It is best to present your stories or case studies to engage the audience in a virtual presentation by including text, graphics, animations, illustrations, diagrams, and schematics. This approach can help the audience understand abstract and complex ideas.

Gendelman encourages presenters to focus on delivery and not just on content. He wants presenters to stick to a schedule and structure the talk for maximum impact.

In a virtual presentation, repetition is important. You can switch from your multimedia presentation to an electronic whiteboard and then have a final review in a chat or polling feature.

Finally, you can integrate a webcam into the presentation. As always, remember to test everything so that you feel confident that the audio and video transmission will work.[5]

Blended Learning Presentations

The high-stakes presentation of choice in the future will take the best of the traditional face-to-face presentation and incorporate more of the virtual presentation and its technical components to give the audience a blended learning experience in real time. It will also provide effective communication and collaboration options so the audience can interact more easily and give feedback to the presenter.

Besides better feedback, it will help organizations communicate across cultures, cross global boundaries, and bring together diverse people with the same mutual interests.

High-stakes presenters of the future will take on more of the role of coaches and less of that of traditional public speakers. They will guide audiences with rhetorical approaches and best practices that will help organizations arrive at solutions that are sustainable, and merit based.

© Rawpixel.com/Shutterstock

The design of blended presentations can take many forms:

1. Visuals will rule content and should be of high quality and offer interesting ideas, concepts, and solutions.
2. Audiences should have some advance materials sent electronically to tablets or phones for easy viewing.
3. Other information and articles should be made available as resource material to support the presentation. This information can be sent directly to audience members electronically or in streaming video format.
4. Speakers should use a conversational tone to facilitate the sharing of ideas rather than the formal tone of a traditional presentation.
5. The audience should be provided with novel solutions that can be applied immediately, not in some far distant future.

The blended learning presentation model can be enhanced with VR, where the visual perception is replaced by a digital one with the help of a headset and controllers. In contrast, AR in a blended presentation includes the merging of the digital and physical worlds, where a user can see the physical space around them (through a lecture or screen). The blended learning presentation can benefit from immersive technology systems that blur the lines between the physical and simulated world.

Finally, there is mixed reality (MR), where the group or hybrid experience is described. One example might be an architect building a home and then moving through it digitally. The advantage of this approach is that the audience can view the home as it is being built.[6]

Summary

1. The future of high-stakes presentations is being shaped by face-to-face, virtual, and blended learning approaches.
2. Trends to watch for in future presentations include learning to communicate data clearly, projection mapping, using VR to create an immersive experience, narrating the audience journey, and adding movie-related content.
3. According to Malcolm Knowles, the success of large face-to-face presentations hinges on the platform itself, the audience, and the relationship between the two.
4. Virtual presentations are starting to play a more significant role in high-stakes scenarios for organizations.
5. New technologies such as artificial intelligence (AI), VR, AR, and MR will help high-stakes presenters give more dramatic and immersive presentations.

Exercises

1. Explain how face-to-face, virtual, and blended learning presentations are shaping the role of high-stakes presentations in organizational settings.
2. What are some trends to watch for in future presentations?
3. How will new technologies such as AI, VR, AR, and MR improve how presenters share ideas with audiences?

Notes

1. Robert J. Petrausch, "Transformative Learning in Toastmasters International" (Ed. D diss., Teachers College, Columbia University, 2002), 160–64.
2. Malcolm Knowles, "Applying Principles of Adult Learning in Conference Presentations," *Adult Learning* 4, no. 1 (September/October 1992): 11–12.
3. Alexa Harrison, *Industry Trends to Watch in 2018*, *www.duarte.com/presentation-skills-resources/presentation*. Retrieved October 14, 2019.
4. Roger Courville, "Perfect Your Virtual Presentation," *The Journal of the American Management Association*, MWorld (Summer 2011).

5. Joel Gendelman, *Virtual Presentations that Work* (New York: McGraw-Hill, 2010), 41, 85, 102, 109.

6. Presentation Studio, *Presenting Our Partners Series, Presenting a New Reality,* June 12, 2018/Technology, *www.presentationstudio.com/blog.* Retrieved October 19, 2019.